Penguin
LIVES

George Herbert Walker Bush

A LIPPER™/ VIKING BOOK

TOM WICKER

George Herbert Walker Bush

A Penguin Life

A LIPPER™/ VIKING BOOK

VIKING
Published by the Penguin Group
Penguin Group (USA) Inc., 375 Hudson Street,
New York, New York 10014, U.S.A.
Penguin Books Ltd, 80 Strand, London WC2R 0RL, England
Penguin Books Australia Ltd, 250 Camberwell Road, Camberwell,
Victoria 3124, Australia
Penguin Books Canada Ltd, 10 Alcorn Avenue,
Toronto, Ontario, Canada M4V 3B2
Penguin Books India (P) Ltd, 11 Community Centre, Panchsheel Park,
New Delhi–110 017, India
Penguin Group (NZ) Ltd, Cnr Airborne and Rosedale Roads, Albany,
Auckland, 1310, New Zealand
Penguin Books (South Africa) (Pty) Ltd, 24 Sturdee Avenue,
Rosebank, Johannesburg 2196, South Africa

Penguin Books Ltd, Registered Offices:
80 Strand, London WC2R 0RL, England

First published in 2004 by Viking Penguin,
a member of Penguin Group (USA) Inc.

1   3   5   7   9   10   8   6   4   2

LIBRARY OF CONGRESS CATALOGING-IN-PUBLICATION DATA
Wicker, Tom.
George Herbert Walker Bush / Tom Wicker.
p.   cm.—(A Penguin life)
Includes bibliographical references.
ISBN 0-670-03303-0
1. Bush, George, 1924–   2. Presidents—United States—Biography.
I. Title.   II. Penguin lives series.
E882.W53 2004
973.928'092—dc22
[B}   2003057633

To Arthur M. Schlesinger Jr.

Friend and Inspiration

George Herbert Walker Bush

PROLOGUE

NOT LONG AFTER George Herbert Walker Bush, the forty-first president of the United States, left office in 1993 and returned to Texas, an old acquaintance found himself at loose ends in Houston. Out of courtesy and curiosity, he called on the former president at his retirement office in the city's federal building.

Cordially and immediately, as befitted long association, the old acquaintance was ushered into a replica of the president's Oval Office in the White House. George Bush, known to family and friends as "Poppy," sat smiling behind a huge executive desk on which there was not a scrap of paper—not a note, a letter, or even a message slip.

While the two men chatted inconsequentially, the former president with his usual grace and friendliness, the phone never rang; no buzzer disturbed the conversation; no secretary or clerk opened the door; no request or notice of any kind was placed on the empty desktop. Their talk of old times was interrupted only when Bush escorted his visitor to a window and pointed out a house he and the former first lady were building in a nearby Houston neighborhood.

"Well, Mister President," Bush's friend finally thought it proper to say, "I just wanted to say hello, but now I'm afraid I'm taking too much of your time."

"No, no!" his host exclaimed. "You're not taking too much time at all. I'm really enjoying our conversation."

Whereupon the old acquaintance stayed for another session of pleasant small talk, during which—again—no sign of any other activity appeared in the ersatz Oval Office. It finally dawned on the visitor that the former president of the United States could take so much time with him because—like thousands of former executives who had retired full of years and honor—he had *nothing else to do*. But surely a man who had spent most of his life in high government office, including a term in the White House—who had in fact presided over the end of the Cold War—must have many ideas and plans, now that his time was his own?

Many years before, the old friend remembered, he and George H. W. Bush had served together on the board of trustees of Phillips Andover Academy, of which they were alumni. During their long joint tenure, the man who would later be president was popular, a helpful figure to his colleagues, supportive of their ideas, willing to take on any task asked of him, doing such jobs well—but he had put forth not a single serious proposal of his own, or any weighty opinion, or even a significant statement. On the Andover board Bush had not seemed to want or need to do anything in particular for the school; he had offered no plans to improve its performance or the lives of its students—just as now, in the Houston Oval Office, behind the clean desk, the former president seemed to have nothing urgent on his mind.

As the visitor finally departed, despite hearty exhortations to stay and talk some more, he could not help wondering if that pleasant hour and his memories from Andover suggested a sort of caretaker mentality—if during George H. W. Bush's life and presidency he had seldom had stronger purposes than he had disclosed on the Andover board, or revealed needs more pressing than maintaining gracious relations with his friends—except, of course, what must have been a burning desire to become president of the United States.

CHAPTER ONE

GEORGE HERBERT WALKER BUSH* based his presidential campaigns on his extensive résumé as a leader of experience and character. Like Dwight D. Eisenhower before him, Bush, as was pointed out by the historian Michael Beschloss, did not offer himself as a proponent of certain issues or of a definite ideology or of any particular policy—such as, say, helping most Americans achieve affordable health care.[1]

In a long prepresidential political career, Bush often used family and political connections to accumulate the experience that supposedly qualified him for the White House. Despite an almost sacrificial devotion to the Republican Party, he sometimes exhibited chameleonlike changes of coloration within its spectrum of opinion, and never overcame the suspicions of its most conservative elements. Throughout Bush's political life, however, his willingness to take on even thankless jobs and his ability to do them well, together with his gift for friendship and his loyalty to the countless friends he had made and kept—sometimes to the point of political risk—lay at the core of his achievement.

*To avoid confusion, all references to "Bush" or "George Bush" in this book will be to George H. W. Bush, the forty-first president. His son, the forty-third president, will be referred to as "George W. Bush," "George junior," or, occasionally, "Junior."

George Bush, the public man, was preeminently the product of family, friendship, his sense of loyalty, his capacity for service—and the patronage of three presidents.

Bush's patrician background, combined with his propensity for verbal stumbles (once, when recalling being shot down over the Pacific during World War II, he concluded: "Lemme tell ya, that'll make you start to think about the separation of church and state"[2]), earned him from Governor Ann Richards of Texas in 1992 the stinging remark that he had been born with "a silver foot in his mouth." Four years later Bush got revenge of a sort when his son George W. Bush defeated Richards's reelection attempt. But the foot was silver indeed; Bush's father was Senator Prescott Bush, Republican of Connecticut, formerly president of Buckeye Steel Castings Co. in Ohio, later a vice president of the New York brokerage firm Brown Brothers Harriman, a founder of the USO during World War II, a president of the U.S. Golf Association, and a frequent golfing companion of President Eisenhower.

In 1921 Prescott Bush married Dorothy Walker, the daughter of George H. Walker, a wealthy businessman, sports enthusiast, and founder of the Walker Cup for golfers. Dorothy was a tennis champion herself and the favored daughter in a highly competitive family. As Mrs. Prescott Bush, she became the mother of five children, the second and favorite of whom, born January 12, 1924, was George Herbert Walker Bush (named for "Dottie's" hard-charging father). George Bush grew up steeped in sports in Greenwich, Connecticut, and spent most summers even more deeply immersed in sports (land and water) at grandfather George H. Walker's 176-acre estate on the seashore at Kennebunkport, Maine.

Not unnaturally, therefore, grandson George H. W. Bush "prepped" at Andover, intending to follow his father to Yale. But after the Japanese attacked Pearl Harbor on December 7, 1941 ("a date that will live in infamy," President Franklin Roosevelt intoned when asking Congress for a declaration of war), seventeen-year-old George ignored whatever family tradition and connections might have done for him. On his eighteenth birthday, January 12, 1942, he was sworn into the U.S. Navy, in a speedup program to train flyers. After earning his wings in less than a year, he became the youngest aviator in the navy.

More than two years later, on September 7, 1944, after Bush had flown numerous missions off the baby flattop *San Jacinto*, his torpedo bomber took a solid hit while flying through heavy flak to attack the island of Chichi Jima. Bush dropped his bomb load to complete the mission, then kept the clumsy old Avenger briefly aloft—long enough to give the crew a chance to bail out. But one of them was trapped aboard; another's chute failed to open; and in the end, like Ishmael, Bush "escaped alone to tell thee." Two hours later his raft was fished out of the water by the submarine *Finback*; typically, he reports in a campaign biography, even aboard the *Finback*, "I made friendships that have lasted a lifetime."[3]

Bush's war was not yet over. He rejoined his squadron in the Philippines for three more months of combat missions (he logged a total of fifty-eight for the war), and finally, in December 1944—three years after Pearl Harbor—was sent home wearing the Distinguished Flying Cross. A few months later, soon after American A-bombs dropped on Hiroshima and Nagasaki ended the war in the summer of 1945, he was a civilian again.

Demobilization meant much the same to George Bush as to

millions of other young Americans who had fought and survived the "good war"—college on the GI Bill (in his case, Yale in
September 1945), enjoying civilian life, and marriage. Two weeks
after his return to the States, Bush married an old girlfriend, Barbara Pierce (his downed plane had been named "Barbara") in
Rye, New York. Their union has lasted for fifty-seven years and
produced six children* (including two sons who became state
governors: George junior of Texas, sworn in as the forty-third
president of the United States in 2001, and Jeb of Florida).

After getting his "ruptured duck" (a pin signifying a discharged
veteran) in the summer of 1945, Bush finally matriculated at
Yale. As might have been expected from his family heritage, he
excelled in athletics (as captain and first baseman of the college
baseball team that played for but lost the national title in 1947
and 1948) and was chosen for the exclusive social society Skull
and Bones; he also did well in his studies, being elected to Phi
Beta Kappa. He and Barbara could celebrate the birth of George
junior, their first child, in July 1946; they "made some close and
lasting friendships" while living off campus in New Haven;[4] and
they seem to have avoided the liberal activism that so frustrated
George's fellow student William F. Buckley Jr.[†]

Bush then joined many another young World War II veteran
as part of a significant postwar migration out of the cities into
the suburbs, and from the old northern industrial belt into the
South and West. At much the same time, thousands of blacks—

*One of whom, daughter Robin, died in 1953 at the age of three.
[†]As recounted in Buckley's *God and Man at Yale* (Chicago: Regnery,
1951).

superseded by the mechanical cotton-picking machine—were moving in the other direction: out of the sharecrop South into old industrial cities like Detroit, Chicago, and Baltimore. The major long-term results of these contramigrations included changes in the nature of such cities, including the growth of black ghettos, and the gradual transformation of the old "Solid South," a Democratic stronghold since Reconstruction following the Civil War, into first a two-party and ultimately a new Republican "Solid South."

After graduation from Yale, Bush decided not to apply for a Rhodes Scholarship on the strange grounds that his small family could not afford to live in England (although he had three thousand dollars[5] in savings from the navy, a not inconsiderable sum in the forties). If this meant that he did not want to call on Bush or Walker family wealth, neither did he turn easily to family business connections. After Procter & Gamble, the big soap company, turned him down, he declined an opportunity to work with his father (and the prominent Democrat Averell Harriman) at Brown Brothers Harriman, and he also rejected an offer from G. H. Walker and Company, his grandfather's private Wall Street banking firm. But enough was enough; Prescott Bush, a member of the board of directors of Dressen Industries, a Texas oil-drilling supply company, then intervened.

Prescott's old friend Henry Neil Mallon, Dressen's president (for whom George and Barbara later named their youngest son), was a sort of "surrogate and father confessor" to Prescott's children.[6] Mallon offered the well-bred young Yalie a lowly clerkship at Ideco, a Dressen subsidiary, in Odessa, Texas (somewhere, as most easterners might have thought, between Kennebunkport and the moon). The booming oil industry looked good, however, and—like millions of other veterans who were pulling up their roots—George H. W. Bush seized the opportunity to begin a new life. Save for a brief transfer to California, the patrician New Englander was to make the rest of his business career—and the beginnings of his political life—in flourishing, boastful Texas.

Bravely, optimistically, he drove south in the new Studebaker his father had given him as a graduation gift, to a new and promising life. "Bar," as Bush always called his wife, and George junior waited at the Walker's Point estate in Kennebunkport until George found a house for them in Odessa—half of a divided "shotgun" structure, with a shared bathroom, on East Seventh Street. They flew to Texas, not only to a different life but to a strange land—drilling rigs, the smell of oil everywhere, and a culture of young would-be entrepreneurs, among whom there was a kind of classless, fences-down comradeship not common among wealthier, more privileged families in the East, even Bushes and Walkers. Above all, however, postwar Texas was perfumed with the sweet scent of opportunity.

George Bush, though he took to his Ideco duties readily enough, was not long in following that scent. Why not, with his connections? At first he had little status—as a rich-kid hired hand from the East, not yet in the promising lease-and-drill business. But, as always, he made friends quickly, and lots of them—with one of whom, a more experienced neighbor named John Overbey, he soon formed Bush-Overbey Oil Development Company. The new firm was partially financed by Brown Brothers, and old George H. Walker himself put in five hundred thousand dollars; other investors, reassured by Prescott Bush's senatorial stature, included Eugene Meyer, publisher of the *Washington*

Post. Prescott's son was on his way—no longer a mere wage worker but part owner of a new player in the sky's-the-limit Texas oil game.

Bush-Overbey did well, and things were beginning to look up for the transplanted Bushes in their intriguing new world, when three-year-old Robin Bush, the little family's secondborn, was diagnosed in 1953 with incurable leukemia. Barbara Bush and the distraught father—probably never before, or at least since his two hours on a raft in the Pacific, faced with a situation about which he could do nothing—still tried to do what they could. They provided Robin with the best medical care in Texas and New York; they tried experimental drugs; they authorized a last-hope surgery—but none of it worked. Robin died a few weeks short of her fourth birthday.

At first it seemed that Barbara Bush could not survive the blow. Though she had suffered Robin's illness in stoic silence, her daughter's death seemed, finally, too much. So lost was she in her grief that she appeared not to want to go on. In later years she often said that, in those terrible times, George Bush saved her—with his never-ending faith and optimism, his assurances that life had to go on, his ability to keep moving, go ahead. Life was still good, he believed, and it was certainly for the living.

Typically, when they came back from the East and Robin's death to Midland, Texas (where, after their brief side assignment to California, they'd moved, into a boxlike house in a tract called Easter Egg Row), George Bush took his wife first to their friends' houses, scattered around town, to thank them for their help and concern during Robin's illness.[7]

It's impossible for parents completely to get over the death of a child. But recovering from Robin's death was easier (though never easy) for George Bush than for his wife, because at about that time he was moving beyond Bush-Overbey. He'd been making friends with one of the boldest and brightest wannabe entrepreneurs in the Texas oil patch—Hugh Lietke Jr.—a Harvard Business School graduate and the son of a well-connected oil-company lawyer in Tulsa, Oklahoma. Lietke saw in Bush, if not a lot of business experience, the great virtue of access to eastern money. And both were willing to take risks—at that time the name of the game in the Texas oil business.

Lietke raised half a million dollars, Bush-Overbey put in the same, and they merged into a single company called Zapata Petroleum—after the Mexican revolutionary portrayed by Marlon Brando in a movie then being shown in Midland. Bush was Zapata's vice president, and half the money had come from his and his family's connections, but contemporary observers in Texas never doubted that Hugh Lietke, with his brains and experience, made most of the decisions.

Whoever deserves the credit, one of those decisions led to a ten-strike. Zapata laid out $850,000—close to its total capital—to lease a huge stretch of land in Coke County, to the east of which Sun Oil had producing wells. If the oil pool Sun was tapping extended to the west, Zapata might have a winner. If it didn't—well, risk *was* the name of the game. But betting nearly everything in one plunge, as Zapata had done, was unusual even in those days in Texas. The partners, moreover, had to put down at least another hundred thousand dollars to drill their first well. If it didn't come in . . . but it did.

So did the next well they drilled. And the next. They drilled seventy-one holes in the Coke County lease—and every one poured black gold out of the Texas earth. By the end of 1953 Zapata was pumping more than a thousand barrels of oil a day, worth at the time more than a million dollars a year. Later even more wells produced even more oil, and the Zapata partners became the first Midland independents to reach a net worth of one million dollars apiece.

John Overbey was not one of them. Hardly a corporate type, he had dropped out of Zapata before the Coke County wells brought in their gushers of wealth (but of course he and George Bush—ever loyal to an old friend—remained close). Newly flush, Bush expanded, investing some of his Zapata gains in a partnership that opened a new business, the Commercial Bank and Trust Company. For his family, money meant a succession of new and bigger houses and what was probably the first backyard swimming pool anybody in the Midland crowd ever had built— a great place for George Bush's many friends to gather at the end of a hot and profitable Texas day.[8]

Bush's career as an entrepreneur continued to flourish with Zapata Petroleum during the 1950s—but underneath financial success he was suffering the gnawing feeling, perhaps bred of Prescott Bush's teachings and example, that he should be giving something back, doing something for the community that was so richly rewarding him.

That attitude had little to do with the division of Zapata in 1958; the problem, if there was one, was more nearly that Hugh Lietke was interested in production and corporate acquisitions while Bush preferred the more adventurous, risk-taking aspects of the oil business. So the 1958 split was a natural. They spun off a second company, called Zapata Offshore, to dig wells in the ocean floor; and George Bush—who believed that undersea drilling was where the future lay—bought the new firm from his partners, became its president, and moved to Houston.

The remains of the original Zapata Petroleum continued to prosper mightily; Hugh Lietke eventually controlled Pennzoil. But most of the eastern money and influence Bush had brought to Texas went with him to Zapata Offshore. G. H. Walker & Company underwrote most of Offshore's public offerings. Its legal work was done by Endicott Davison, a Skull and Bonesman with George Bush at Yale in 1948. Even the Texas company that underwrote the initial stock issue, Underwood, Neuhaus, had an old Andover classmate, Robert Parish, on its staff. And when a Gulf hurricane blew away one of Offshore's three-million-dollar oil rigs,* G. H. Walker and Company quietly handled the financial side of the matter back east. On the scene in Houston, George Bush proved a competent manager—and, in his usual pattern, made lots of new friends, some of them influential.

On its fifth anniversary, Offshore was listed on the American Stock Exchange and had attracted twenty-two hundred stockholders. The company occupied offices in the Houston Club building, had a fleet of four monster drilling rigs, employed 195 people, carried an impressive load of debt, and enjoyed plenty of business either under way or pending[9]—including operations on Cay Sal Bank in the eastern Gulf of Mexico, once leased by Howard Hughes. Meanwhile, not least as a result of the huge so-

---

*Three-legged, weighing nine million pounds each, and built by R. G. LeTourneau of Vicksburg, Mississippi. Bush, *Looking Forward*, pp. 70–71.

cial and political migrations in which George Bush had partici-pated, Texas was metamorphosing from safely Democratic into something approaching a two-party state.*

Governor Allan Shivers had led a "Democrats for Eisen-hower" movement in 1952, and Texas was one of five southern states Ike carried that year. The growth of the Texas GOP—fueled by oil wealth, the influx of outsiders, and the state's basi-cally conservative electorate—continued in the fifties. By 1961, when Lyndon Johnson abandoned his Senate seat to become vice president of the United States, Texas elected John Tower as his replacement—the state's first Republican senator since Re-construction.

In that special election Tower had benefited from being the only Republican in the field with seventy-five Democrats, in-cluding Bing Crosby's father-in-law. Texas Democrats also were somewhat complacent, sure they could defeat Tower one-on-one in the regular election of 1962 if he managed to win in 1961. As things turned out, he survived both elections and went on to win three more terms, and to be nominated for secretary of de-fense by President George H. W. Bush in 1989.

A signal part of the Texas party's growth, however, was an archconservative sector in the image of, and deeply devoted to, Barry Goldwater, the guru of the swiftly emerging national con-servative movement. When the Harris County (Houston) Re-publican chairman moved to Florida in 1962, the right-wing John Birch Society was strong enough to threaten a takeover of

*Cay Sal Bank was reportedly sometimes used as a base for CIA raids into Castro's Cuba. In 1981, when Bush became vice president of the United States, all Securities and Exchange Commission filings for Zapata Offshore, 1960–66, were destroyed.

the county Republican committee. That's when leading Harris County Republicans asked the prosperous businessman and popular Houston resident George Bush to run for the chairmanship; and that's when Prescott Bush's restless son saw the opportunity for community service that he'd been seeking—never mind that Zapata Offshore required of him as much management effort as one man could reasonably handle.

Bush proved a roaring success, the hardest-working chairman Harris County Republicans ever had seen. He was enthusiastic and optimistic, raised money, organized precincts, brought in recruits, found volunteers, computerized the voter rolls, moved the committee to better quarters, and stayed right on top of the paperwork. In his new role he again made lots of new friends; women Republicans especially liked his good looks, his unfailing courtesy. Under Bush's committee leadership, the party even elected Houston's first Republican city councilman.

Everything Chairman Bush touched seemed to succeed—except that he could never win the Birchers' friendship, hard as he tried, not even when he named some of them to leadership positions in the county. He was too eastern, too Yale, too moderate, the epitome of everything Barry Goldwater was not—or so the Birchers were convinced. In 1963, nevertheless, Bush saw the kind of tempting opportunity that might offer him a political success similar to Offshore's in business; he determined to seek the Republican nomination to run in 1964 against Texas's senior senator—the old populist liberal Ralph Yarborough.

Bush believed that Yarborough was out of touch with a Texas grown more conservative since the senator's last election. Owing to Bush's own labors among Republicans, he also believed that the state was tired of the old man. Even Lyndon Johnson was believed to have little use for Yarborough. And with Goldwater given a good chance to be nominated for president and to carry Texas for the Republicans, he might well bring in an attractive Republican senate candidate on his coattails. All in all a race against Ralph Yarborough looked like a pretty good bet for a young man—Bush would be only forty in 1964—who was obviously going places.

He threw himself without stint into a four-candidate Republican primary, helped by the zealous work of his wife and eldest son, George W.—eighteen years old in 1964—and by all those Houston volunteers he had organized and led so enthusiastically. Bush was a poor speaker with a tinny voice—but he was a splendid handshaker, backslapper, and fresh face, a man never too busy or too tired, moreover, to dash off dozens of thank-you notes daily (probably thousands by the end of the campaign) to anyone who'd helped him in even the smallest way. He was piling up new friendships almost faster than they could be recorded in the card file Barbara Bush relentlessly kept up to date.

Even as a relative newcomer to Texas—naturally Yarborough and Republican primary opponents called him a carpetbagger—Bush led the primary with a plurality, then defeated his main rival in a runoff in which he took more than 60 percent of the vote. That, of course, was only among registered Republicans, of whom there were not yet too many in Texas. Bush not only had still to take on Yarborough himself; he had to confront the uncomfortable fact that Goldwater probably couldn't win Texas after all—because Lyndon Johnson had become president, succeeding the murdered John F. Kennedy, and there was no doubt that LBJ, the master of Texas politics, would be at the top of the Democratic ticket in 1964.

Back in Connecticut, Prescott Bush—retired from the Senate since 1962—was one of those Eisenhower Republicans itching to knock Goldwater out of the Republican running and rescue their party from its fire-breathing right wing. Prescott Bush and other Eisenhower Republicans first favored Nelson Rockefeller of New York, then William Scranton of Pennsylvania—anyone, in fact, but AUH2O (as Goldwater's bumper stickers proclaimed him). Down in Texas, however, George Bush—the Republican Senate nominee but also a relative newcomer from the East, a Yalie, and maybe even an internationalist—realized that if his own father came out publicly against Goldwater, all those Texas right-wingers never reconciled to the son would be newly angered and aroused.

So Prescott Bush received an anguished phone call from George Bush—and thereafter Prescott remained loyally silent, doing nothing throughout 1964 to stop his party from nominating Barry Goldwater for president (to be fair, Dwight Eisenhower himself did little more). In Texas, Bush had recognized that he would sink or swim with Goldwater at the top of the national Republican ticket—and he was neither willing to sink nor at a loss about how to swim. He moved almost as far to the right as was Goldwater himself, then staged another fighting, hand-shaking, note-writing campaign, visiting more than half of Texas's 254 counties (in most of which no Republican organization existed). The supposed eastern moderate one-worlder opposed the Civil Rights Act of 1964, just passed by Congress under LBJ's unique pressures; he denounced the United Nations, deplored what he called the "soft" Democratic policy on the war in Vietnam, and argued against a nuclear test-ban treaty. Three years after the Bay of Pigs fiasco, he even proposed arming Cuban exiles for another go at Fidel Castro.

With a patrician sense of propriety, however, that might seem odd to those of a different background, Bush refused all suggestions that he talk about his wartime heroism. That would be bad form, contrary to the code of sportsmanship that Bush had learned from his grandfather, his mother, and his father, and at Andover: One did not boast about one's accomplishments.

Though Bush was still not much of a stump speaker and had no identifying "message" except the claim, endlessly repeated, that Yarborough was a proven giveaway artist, a liberal out of step with Texas, his campaign—featuring country music, barbecue, a determinedly folksy candidate, and stump speeches from Goldwater and Richard Nixon—clearly was not hopeless, not at first, anyway. Then President Lyndon Johnson, who had little love for Ralph Yarborough but even less for John Tower, and who was determined that his home state would not have *two* Republican senators, swept into Texas, rolled out the political power he had been stockpiling for thirty years, and gathered even Yarborough into his fulsome embrace. In the end, on his way to a national landslide, LBJ took 63 percent of the Texas presidential vote and easily carried Ralph Yarborough back to the Senate. George Bush could take comfort only from the fact that his creditable 44 percent, though swamped by Johnson's huge majority, represented the most votes any Republican had ever won in Texas.

In his book *Looking Forward* Bush does not even mention his right-wing, Goldwaterish performance in 1964, remarking only that his "was the kind of campaign not generally identified with Republican candidates, a leaf taken from the old Texas populist book."[10] In the days following his defeat, however, Bush told his minister in Houston, "I took some far-right positions to get elected. I hope I never do it again. I regret it."[11] The sincerity of this resolve was to be tested again and again in the years to come—years that found George Bush, the successful oilman, devoting himself almost fully to politics and government.

The greatest irony of 1964 may have been that even his taking those "far-right positions" didn't win the John Birchers over to George Bush, any more than his Reaganesque attitudes during his presidency, 1989–93, were to convince conservatives of that later era that he was one of them. In 1964, the Birchers thought they knew a "moderate" when they saw one, no matter what he might be saying to win votes. So they sat on their hands during Bush's campaign and took a walk on election day. Better even Ralph Yarborough than an easterner—probably a closet internationalist to boot.

If luck seemed to have deserted George Bush when Johnson was sworn in as president within an hour of Kennedy's death, Bush's political fortunes were quickly reversed after 1964. As Harris County Republican chairman in 1963, he had filed suit for a redrawing of the county's congressional districts, basing the case on the Supreme Court's one-man, one-vote decision. National population shifts also had enlarged the Texas congressional entitlement. So a new Houston district was created for 1966—white, wealthy, with few Hispanic or black voters but including a lot of newcomers to Texas. Reflecting his changed personal priorities—politics over business—Bush sold his share of Zapata Offshore for more than one million dollars and filed for the seat.

As the Republican candidate who had done well in the losing cause against LBJ and Ralph Yarborough, Bush had good "name recognition" and rather easily won the House seat in a contest with Houston's Democratic district attorney, Frank Briscoe—

who made the mistake of calling his opponent a carpetbagger in a district full of carpetbaggers. But even with Bush's gifts for friendship, his indexed filing cases of friends, and the advantages of the new constituency, the new congressman was not solely responsible for his victory. In 1966 a new tide was running, led nationally by Richard Nixon. Republicans rebounded from the Goldwater debacle of two years earlier, taking sixty-six House seats—including the new Houston Seventh. There, both Nixon and House Republican leader Gerald Ford had campaigned personally for that promising newcomer—Prescott Bush's son George.

(The 1966 results, not incidentally, paved the way for Nixon's nomination and comeback presidential campaign in 1968, and thus indirectly—as will be seen—for George Bush's own national political career.)

Rather inexplicably Bush recorded in *Looking Forward* that "a disappointing aspect" of the 1966 vote was "my being swamped in the black precincts, despite . . . an all-out effort to attract black voters."[12] Can he have forgotten that he had opposed the Civil Rights Act of 1964 in his right-wing campaign against Ralph Yarborough? Or did he believe that blacks should know that a Yale-educated candidate of good family could not be racially biased and was for them in his heart, no matter how political circumstances might have forced him to vote?

In other ways the Seventh District campaign yielded political connections to match the family position Bush already had. As one of forty-seven freshman Republicans in the House, he managed a coup—membership on the important Ways and Means Committee, an impossible feat for most rookies and unknowns without a father who'd served in the Senate. Otherwise his first term was undistinguished except for his typically hard work for his constituents and his assiduous courting of even the least among them (the name cards kept piling up in Barbara's files).

In 1968 he scored a politician's dream—reelection unopposed, in some ways a reward for his good record. Almost as important, Nixon—Bush's benefactor in 1964 and 1966—moved into the White House in early 1969. Bush's name even turned up on a leaked shortlist of those Nixon supposedly was considering as his vice presidential choice (which doesn't necessarily mean that Bush was actually a serious contender, or a contender at all; but the mere report helped along his embryonic political career). Nixon later told him, "I really couldn't pick a one-term congressman."[13]

Bush had, however, near the end of his first term, when he knew he would have no opponent for 1968, cast one controversial vote—in favor of one of the last gasps of Lyndon Johnson's Great Society, an open-housing bill.* Though he'd expected criticism, the uproar of surprise and anger in his wealthy white district surprised him. The backlash couldn't hurt him in 1968, since he was running unopposed—but that vote would not be forgotten in Houston and Texas.

In 1970 it was one of the reasons Bush's luck turned bad again. That year, he was pondering whether to give up his safe House seat and take on Senator Yarborough a second time. A foolish move? Actually there seemed little risk. Bush was popular, a leader of the emerging Texas Republican Party; Yarborough really had outstayed his Texas welcome by 1970; and, anyway,

---

*To prevent housing discrimination against blacks and others by real estate agents and landlords.

Richard Nixon told Bush in urging him to run that he'd be considered for a high-level administration job in the unlikely event he should lose.

Even former President Johnson, his old antipathy to Ralph Yarborough apparently aroused again, gave Bush veiled encouragement. The congressman had had the good sense—and political perspicacity—to go to Andrews Air Force Base to see Johnson off to Texas when LBJ left the presidency in 1969. Now Bush called at the LBJ Ranch and asked Johnson, not if he'd support him, but if he thought Bush should give up the House seat for a Senate run.

LBJ replied that he'd served in the House and the Senate, that he wouldn't advise Bush what to do, but he would say that "the difference between being a member of the Senate and a member of the House is the difference between chicken salad and chicken shit." After this typically Johnsonian, only slightly Delphic remark, he asked: "Do I make my point?"[14]

With everything looking so promising, Bush not unnaturally opted for chicken salad and filed for the Senate race. But he was to be handed, in LBJ's graphic description, a plate of chicken shit. Old Senator Yarborough lost his party's primary to a more conservative Democrat, a former congressman named Lloyd Bentsen—a protégé of Governor John Connally (who was still a Democrat in 1970) and a man Lyndon Johnson could and did openly support. Suddenly, his bridges burned, George Bush no longer had an elderly, worn-out opponent, a "liberal giveaway artist." Instead he faced a tough, vigorous, conservative Democrat in what was still mostly a conservative Democratic state. He was no longer likely to go to the Senate his father once had graced, and he had given up even the prospect of going back to the House.

Nevertheless, with his usual zeal and enthusiasm, Bush pitched headlong into the race against Bentsen—this time positioning himself to the left of his opponent (despite his earlier pledge to that minister not to take positions again just to get votes). He ran as the more liberal of the two candidates, even reaching out to blacks and Hispanics, building on the open-housing vote.

He may have had little choice, but the tactic was questionable anyway. Bush was no longer running in his familiar Houston district but statewide—in a state in which more whites were opposed to or suspicious of open housing and liberalism than minorities were for them. Those who'd voted for Ralph Yarborough in the primary remembered how Bush had savaged the old man in 1964, and most stayed with Bentsen. Nixon came to Texas in full cry and skewered the Democrats—dooming any Bush hope for a crossover vote. Bentsen tabbed him repeatedly as "a liberal Ivy League carpetbagger," and this time the charge struck a damaging note in Texas—and stuck to Bush for years. Representative Jim Wright, Democrat of Texas and Speaker of the House, once mocked Bush at a Gridiron Club dinner as "the only Texan . . . who eats lobster with his chili" and "had a downhome quiche cook-off."[15]

Even so Bush went down fighting, bettering his 1964 vote percentage; but 46 percent was still not good enough. Bentsen went to the Senate, ultimately to a vice presidential candidacy and to become secretary of the treasury under President Bill Clinton. George Bush was not to win an election on his own for another eighteen years. Barbara Bush and the family wept; but George went right back to work, phoning and writing to those who had helped him.

There were a lot of people to be thanked, a lot of new friends, a good sign for the future if you were as optimistic as George Bush usually was. But on the sad night when the votes were counted in 1970, even he must have realized that little remained of what had been a surging political career—except Richard Nixon's pledge of a job in the national administration.

CHAPTER TWO

THE TROUBLE WAS that Nixon's promise was not exactly a pledge; the president had offered only a general assurance that Bush believed he could rely on. Nor had Nixon offered or even suggested any particular job. But from election day in November 1970 until Bush's second congressional term and his service in the House ended in January 1971, he could personally seek the president's ear.

He returned to Washington after the campaign against Bentsen not certain—by his own testimony—whether he wanted to go back to Texas or stay in Washington, the latter only if a specific offer from Nixon proved attractive. Charles Bartlett, the Washington correspondent of the *Chattanooga* Times (Bush's close personal friend and formerly John F. Kennedy's), touted to him the idea of being ambassador to the United Nations. Perhaps stimulated by Bartlett, a well-known figure in Washington, Secretary of State William Rogers also talked to the lame-duck Congressman about the UN post.[1]

When Nixon's chief of staff, Bob Haldeman, called Bush to the White House on December 9, 1970, however, he suggested primarily that the Texas oilman should become a special assistant to the president; Haldeman also mentioned the chairmanship of the Republican National Committee (RNC)—and the

UN ambassadorship, that idea obviously having gone beyond Charlie Bartlett.

When the president asked Haldeman to join him that day, the chief of staff took Bush into the Oval Office, where the three men chatted for about forty minutes. Bush said he did not want the National Committee job "under existing circumstances"— meaning that he wanted neither to be an "attack dog" for the administration nor to take orders from aggressive White House staffers like Charles Colson (who later served jail time for his White House activities). Bush suggested, however, that the UN job had "real appeal" because he believed he "could spell out [Nixon's] programs with some style" and "put forward an image" really helpful to the administration. Nixon was impressed; he probably realized by then not only George Bush's family advantages but his talent for making and keeping friends. He decided to appoint Bush a special White House assistant while ordering Secretary Rogers to "put a hold" on the UN appointment. But fifteen minutes after Bush got back to his Capitol Hill office, Haldeman called; Nixon had talked to Rogers immediately, and they were "ready to go" with George Bush as ambassador to the United Nations.[2]

Apparently the president had liked the notion of having the stylish, gregarious ex-congressman, boasting the kind of family background and connections that Nixon secretly envied, represent him in New York and on the UN version of the world scene. And anyway, Nixon and the incumbent ambassador, Charles Yost, a career diplomat, were not comfortable with each other. On December 11, 1970, scarcely a month after Lloyd Bentsen had shown Bush the exit door from Texas politics, the defeated senatorial candidate was appointed ambassador to the UN to replace Yost—evoking the predictable outrage of those who perceived that an experienced diplomat had been dumped in favor of a lame-duck politician.

Bush himself believed that Nixon considered the ambassadorship "as much . . . a political as a diplomatic assignment," and was therefore confident that Bush's political experience, however limited, would be an asset offsetting his lack of foreign affairs experience. The new ambassador, moreover, considered himself an advocate—"not an apologist"—for Nixon's policies at the "glass palace" and was too wise in the ways of government to expect to be a policy maker.[3]

He was also ready and able to deploy his innate talent for winning new friends in new surroundings at the UN. He had studied the issues well and represented the nation ably; Barbara Bush was an adept and outgoing partner, courting delegates' wives as he pursued the delegates themselves. After hours the Bushes entertained colleagues eagerly, and they were of course a social success in New York, among many old acquaintances. And they lived well in the ambassador's big, plush apartment at the Waldorf Astoria (a long way from Easter Egg Row in Texas). The good life in New York was darkened, however, when Prescott Bush became a lung cancer patient at Manhattan's Sloan-Kettering Memorial Hospital. He died on October 8, 1972.

Bush quickly made a genial impression among the other UN representatives. Many of them, having slowly made their way up the ladder in their home governments, were still to be friends years later—powerful friends, foreign ministers, even prime ministers. When George Bush became president of the United States in 1989, these old acquaintances were among his main assets.

At the UN he was not, however, always able to count other

nations' representatives as new friends. He was not overly surprised, for instance, to find that in his first experience of stone-faced Soviet diplomacy, his sunny personality did him little good. The very first Security Council meeting he attended was forced by Yakov Malik, the Soviet Union's ambassador and a master of "diplomatic" hostility. Malik wanted to talk about the pace of Israeli withdrawal from Palestinian territory, which had only slowly—if at all—followed the Six-Day War of 1967; he complained loudly and rudely that the United States was taking orders from Israel. In *Looking Forward* Bush portrays himself as cool and calm under this first burst of fire, telling Malik that the charge was too "ridiculous" to deserve an answer.[4] This Cold War exchange foreshadowed almost constant conflict between the two ambassadors throughout Bush's two years at the UN.

(Typically, however, when Malik was recalled to the Soviet Union in 1976, Bush—by then director of the CIA—wrote him a warm note, concluding: "Someday maybe I will get a chance to visit Moscow—if I do maybe I can get you to buy me a glass of vodka. So long, my friend, good luck. George."[5])

In those years the so-called Third World nations—those considered underdeveloped or "developing" and not necessarily officially committed to either the Soviet Union or the United States—were gradually becoming a majority in the General Assembly; "little wiener nations," Bush privately called them.[6] Automatic U.S. dominance was nearing its end. It fell to Bush, for instance, to cast only the second Security Council veto in American and UN history—in this instance on a 1972 resolution that censured Israel for attacking Palestinian bases in Syria and Lebanon but did not condemn the murder of Israeli athletes at the Munich Olympics.

Despite major lobbying efforts, for another example, Bush and his team in 1971 suffered a stinging defeat and got an acid taste of life in the Nixon administration. In the evolving General Assembly a new Third World majority wanted to expel Taiwan and seat the Beijing (Communist) government of China in its place. Nixon, and therefore Bush, had accepted the inevitability of Beijing in the UN, but Ambassador Bush—following instructions—fought hard for a "dual representation" plan that would maintain Washington's commitment to and relationship with Taiwan. That summer, however, Nixon's national security adviser, Henry Kissinger, made his breakthrough visit to China, and it was announced in Washington that Nixon himself soon would go to Beijing.

These developments pulled the diplomatic rug from under Bush's feet (as, in another context, they also slighted Secretary of State Rogers, who had been kept in the dark) and finished "dual representation" at the UN. How could it be advocated in New York when it was being undercut in Washington?

On the key procedural vote, lost by the United States by only 59 to 55, Bush was stunned again to see several nations he had thought committed to the American and Taiwanese side abstaining, and several others absenting themselves altogether. "I still remember the countries that ... broke their word," Bush, the supposedly experienced political head counter, recalled in 1987— as if such flip-flops never happened in U.S. politics. For George Bush the hard-earned lesson—following the disclosure of Nixon and Kissinger's behind-his-back diplomacy—was that, in the new UN, "Taiwan wasn't really the issue. Kicking Uncle Sam was."[7]

Not long thereafter Bush saw at first hand another new circumstance. At an informal Security Council session in the apartment of France's UN ambassador, the new Chinese representative, Huang Hua, deliberately and ostentatiously refused to shake the proffered hand of Yakov Malik—who "turned a livid shade of purple." With the other Security Council members, Bush was graphically shown, if they didn't already know, that "no matter what the state of détente between the United States and the Soviets, there was another Cold War . . . between the world's two biggest Communist powers."

That lesson was a major reason why the United Nations—aside from its humanitarian activities—left on George Bush the lasting impression that, contrary to the hopes and dreams of idealists, the organization "is and always will be a reflection of, rather than a solution to, the tensions that exist in the world."[8]

He had little opportunity or time to apply such lessons. It's difficult to read the careful phrases of *Looking Forward* without sensing Bush's disappointment when, at Nixon's behest, his relatively brief UN tenure came to an end. Not only was he leaving the glamorous "glass palace"; he was being shunted off to the Republican National Committee—a drastic shift from important world affairs to grubby U.S. politics.

Bush had hoped, with some reason, for something better—Barbara Bush especially so—perhaps for a cabinet appointment, at least at the deputy secretary level. After Nixon's landslide reelection in November 1972, against the weak opposition of George McGovern, the president was apparently thinking of a major government reform: the appointment of a sort of "super-cabinet" that would help him run the administration, while deputies actually handled the activities of the various cabinet departments. At least those like George Bush, who considered themselves "in the know," generally believed that Nixon was thinking along those lines. George Shultz, the secretary of the treasury, actually suggested to Bush that he become Shultz's deputy and run the Treasury Department—Shultz apparently planning to be part of the "super-cabinet."

At Camp David a relaxed Nixon told Bush that Shultz's proposal was all right with him, if that was really what Bush wanted to do. But, the president said pointedly, what *he* really needed was for Bush to run the RNC and, in the next four years, to build a new and stronger Republican Party. With the Watergate problem even then somewhat more than a cloud on the horizon, this vision probably did not overly impress Bush, who had by then compiled a ten-year political career from Houston to the UN.

After thinking things over, however, and seeking advice from Commerce Secretary Rogers Morton and from a former party chairman, Senator Hugh Scott of Pennsylvania, Bush nevertheless decided—reluctantly, he virtually concedes—that he'd do it if given a free hand at the RNC and allowed to sit at the cabinet table. Nixon agreed, after giving Bush his personal assurance that he'd had nothing to do with the Watergate break-in or the subsequent cover-up; so the deal was struck. Bush could console himself with the knowledge that he'd done what the president wanted; and what else could a loyal public servant do when asked from the top?

Another loyal Republican, Senator Bob Dole of Kansas, the RNC chairman Bush would replace, received in this episode his own experience of political grace as understood in the Nixon administration. Not that Dole wanted to keep the job; he knew Watergate was far from over, and, anyway, he had his own reelection in Kansas to seek in 1974. But two weeks after the 1972 landslide, he was summoned to Camp David and a personal interview with the president. A cordial Nixon gave him a jacket that proclaimed "Camp David" on its back and said he knew Dole was ready to move on—a little sooner than Dole himself wanted—and was thinking about George Bush as a replacement. Would Dole go to New York and sound out Bush about the job?

Dole would. He met Ambassador Bush at the Waldorf—their first meeting, though in the future the two men would twice be opposing contenders for the Republican presidential nomination. Bush gave only a noncommittal reply to the RNC idea. Dole dutifully reported this to Nixon—and then learned, but only from a news leak, that he was out and Bush was in as RNC chairman, that in fact Bush had talked with Nixon and accepted the job *before* Dole went to New York ostensibly to sound him out. Bob Dole, faithful Republican and loyal Nixon friend, was left with his "Camp David" jacket and "an unfading memory of Bush's blank, friendly smile" during their meeting at the Waldorf.[9]

George Bush was left with a job he really didn't want and, as he must have anticipated, two big problems. The bullying White House staff to which he had objected in 1971 was mostly still in place in 1973. And an "attack dog" was more than ever needed to head the committee because—contrary to Republicans' and many pundits' predictions—Nixon's reelection had not stilled the growing national outcry over the Watergate scandal. The problem had erupted in June 1972, owing to what the White House had myopically termed "a third-rate burglary" at the offices of the Democratic National Committee,* and had been steadily expanding.

---

*Located in the Watergate apartment building; hence the name that quickly clung to the scandal.

In retrospect it can be seen that Watergate doomed from the start any possibility that George Bush or anyone else might build a new and stronger Republican Party in Nixon's second term. From the time Bush took the RNC chairmanship in early 1973 until Nixon himself was forced to resign, on August 8, 1974, the chairman could focus on little other than the mushrooming Watergate threat. In his first year he logged 97,000 miles of travel to thirty-three states, gave more than a hundred speeches, and held seventy-eight press conferences, not to mention making many television appearances—almost all devoted to the defense of Richard Nixon.

A personal friend of the president and his family, who with his wife had been invited to Tricia Nixon's White House wedding, a man who had often benefited from Nixon's more official patronage and assistance, above all a man reared to value loyalty and duty, Bush was forced to spend most of his time as chairman defending his chief—apparently in the honest belief, so he asserts, that Nixon had committed no culpable offense. Most party chairmen act primarily as cheerleaders; Bush later recalled that his job "was to serve as a bandage carrier, traveling the country to wrap up party wounds."[10]

It was small consolation that he could and did point out to Republicans everywhere that Watergate was not the work of the National Committee—half the staff of which he had fired anyway—but the product of an organization that had functioned independently: CREEP, the acronym for the Committee to Reelect the President. In 1973, as the *New York Times* political correspondent, I was covering a national governors' conference somewhere out west when the beleaguered Republican national chairman arrived on one of those save-the-party missions.

Bush first conferred with the Republican governors, then took me aside—backstage in a cavernous auditorium—to assure me that Nixon was not guilty, that ultimately the charges of the *Times* and other critics would be shown to be unfair and unwarranted. Bush was trying hard, I remember thinking, but was not really convincing—either about Nixon's innocence or about his own belief that the president would survive the scandal. He did concede that the political situation for Nixon and his party was bad and getting worse.

The release of the so-called "smoking gun" tape* in the summer of 1974 apparently persuaded the chairman, like many other Americans, that the president was, and had been, lying about his attempts to cover up his aides' involvement in Watergate. Or perhaps disclosure of the tape only released an inner conviction—or fear—that Bush had been suppressing. In any case it obviously was devastating to learn that Nixon had lied to him personally.

When the president called a cabinet meeting on August 6, 1974, Bush attended and sat in a chair against the wall—an invited guest, not a participant at the table. The meeting proceeded routinely until Attorney General William Saxbe brought up Watergate. Nixon told his colleagues that he would *not* quit, though his resignation was then being widely demanded; he did not believe, he said, that he had committed an impeachable offense, and he did not want to weaken the presidency by resignation.

Gen. Al Haig, who had by then replaced Haldeman as Nixon's

---

*Disclosing that Nixon had acquiesced in Bob Haldeman's cover-up plan for the FBI to stay out of a supposed "national security" incident.

chief of staff, was startled to see that George Bush, from one of the chairs along the wall, was seeking the floor. Nixon did not call on him, but Bush spoke up anyway. Watergate was the vital question, he said; it was sapping public confidence in the president, the party, the economy, the country as a whole. Therefore Nixon *should* resign, the party chairman told the president to his face—while the cabinet and others present sat in shocked silence. Nixon apparently said nothing.[11]

Bush had not been seized by a sudden courageous inspiration. All those visits with party leaders, the volume and tenor of reports he had received from Republicans around the country, the revelations of Senator Sam Ervin's Watergate investigating committee, the disclosures on the president's tapes—all had persuaded Bush, finally, in what has to be seen as one of the least calculated moments of his political life, to *act*, not only against his usual caution and circumspection but against the Walker creed of supporting the team, even to jeopardize his long and close relationship with a friend, a man who had campaigned for him in Texas and awarded him high office at the UN and in Washington.

That same day, August 6, Senator Barry Goldwater of Arizona—whose hapless presidential campaign had ruined George Bush's first Senate candidacy in 1964—led a Republican delegation to the White House to tell Nixon bluntly that he no longer had enough support in the Senate to stave off conviction on impeachment charges. The next day, even on sober second thought, Republican National Chairman George Bush delivered a personal letter to the president, reiterating his "considered judgment that you should now resign"—but declaring too "the gratitude I will always feel toward you."[12]

On August 8, 1984, Richard M. Nixon, under threat of impeachment, became the first, and so far the only, president to resign. George H. W. Bush was high among those who had forced his hand.

Gerald Ford—not even an elected but an appointed vice president*—automatically became president when Nixon's resignation took effect. Ford and Bush had been well acquainted during the latter's two terms in the House, so Bush—perhaps emboldened by having spoken out to Nixon—let the new president know that he'd be interested in taking Ford's old place, now vacant, as vice president.

This might have been a cheeky move for a man who'd never been elected to anything more important than a seat (one of 435) in the House. But it was relatively easy for the party chairman to arrange informal polls of National Committeemen and -women and of Republican members of Congress, both of which paid off: Their choice for the vice presidency turned out to be George H. W. Bush—no doubt the deserved fruit of his assiduous labors in the otherwise unrewarding RNC chairmanship, which had brought him into contact with so many Republicans and new friends.

Ford nevertheless passed over Bush to choose the thrice-thwarted presidential aspirant, Governor Nelson Rockefeller of New York—the most prestigious Republican officeholder but conspicuously *not* the favorite of the ever-more-conservative

---

*Nixon had chosen Ford, the House minority leader, to replace Spiro T. Agnew, who had pleaded *nolo contendere* to the charge of accepting bribes while he was governor of Maryland.

party rank and file. This choice, if not the rejection of George Bush, appears nearly thirty years later to have been a political blunder, however logical at the time, second only to Ford's pardon of Nixon. At any rate in 1976 Ford was forced to ditch Rockefeller, when, as an incumbent president, he sought to succeed himself in the White House (only narrowly defeating Ronald Reagan for the Republican presidential nomination).

Apparently, however, Ford did take seriously Chairman Bush's bid for the briefly open vice presidency. That's attested—at least by Bush in *Looking Forward*—by his claim that the president personally telephoned to give him the bad news. More important, Ford then offered the former congressman, ambassador, and current Republican chairman the choice of two about-to-be-vacant and hugely important foreign embassies—in London and Paris.

Here were heady prospects indeed. After no more than a couple of years at the UN, less than two at the committee, and four in the House—all relatively obscure positions, in political terms—Bush was being offered either of two real foreign-policy prizes. Obviously Prescott Bush's son had made his usual good impression on Ford, in the House and in the presidency—Bush's real gift for friendship, among his other qualities, at work again. Both embassies, of course, needed to be headed by someone of considerable wealth, owing to social demands in Paris and London, and to the State Department's niggardly provisions for foreign service. Bush was not Rockefeller-rich but qualified as a successful oilman with ample links to moneyed friends and family. Still he had no great record of achievement, and Ford must have been impressed with Bush personally to offer such vital posts to a relatively low-ranking political figure.

Bush—though resentful of being passed over for the vice presidency—did not jump at either opportunity, perhaps because he felt the confidence of one who had a long family pedigree, who had had a useful life outside politics and government, and who had made a host of friends, influential and otherwise. He was nevertheless anxious to put distance between himself and the political nightmare of the party chairmanship during the decline and fall of Richard Nixon.

Bush and his wife, moreover, recalled their successful postwar experiment of leaving family and the East for an uncertain future in the Texas oil patch. Now the Far East looked like the same kind of challenge—and held the same kind of promise. Nixon and Kissinger, as Bush had bitter reason to recall, had restored China to high rank on the American foreign-policy agenda; and the U.S.–China relationship would be one of the most important in world affairs in the years ahead. Bush knew, moreover, that David Bruce, the veteran diplomat who then was head of the U.S. Liaison Office in Beijing (the two nations still had no formal diplomatic relations) was planning to leave.

Ford was shocked to learn, therefore, that Bush opted to replace Bruce in China rather than take London or Paris. Shocked, too, was Henry Kissinger, by then secretary of state and the guru of U.S. China policy. "For the most part," Kissinger told Bush, "you'll be bored beyond belief." One reason the secretary thought so was that he and close associates like Philip Habib and Winston Lord not only managed China policy but tightly held information about it among themselves. Bush would find out, as had Bruce, that it took a "bureaucratic battle" even to learn the details of Kissinger's private talks with China's representative in Washington, Huang Zhen.

Nevertheless Ford made the appointment and Kissinger approved, or at least acquiesced. In September 1974, George and Barbara Bush left the national committee and Watergate far behind, no doubt gratefully, and flew to China—a departure perhaps as forward-looking as their postwar move to Texas. Theirs, however, proved to be a largely uneventful thirteen months at the U.S. Liaison Office in Beijing. In *Looking Forward,* the pages that describe Bush's time in China[13] are filled primarily with the trivia of his day-to-day personal life:

- Being told that the "fragrant meat" he and Barbara had eaten at one dinner was, in fact, "the upper lip of a wild dog."
- "Breaking the mold" of U.S. representation in Beijing by attending national-day receptions at various embassies, and riding bicycles instead of using the Chrysler limousine furnished by the Chinese.
- Renewing a Bush-style friendship with Qiao Guanhua, who had been Beijing's representative at the United Nations during Bush's own UN years, and who had risen to become vice minister of foreign affairs (but who would later fall from power for having backed the wrong faction in the internal Chinese political wars).
- A Christmas Day visit to "the caves"—the underground tomb shelters the Chinese had built under Beijing, as a measure to thwart a possible *Soviet*—not American—nuclear attack.
- Daughter Dorothy's christening in a Christian church, attended by the diplomatic corps.

Accounts of important diplomatic events are few and far between—though Bush does record what he regarded as a significant remark by "a high Chinese official" soon after Saigon had fallen to the North Vietnamese. "The United States has a useful role to play in Asia," the official said, in tones that caused Bush to interpret this apparent banality as an authorized diplomatic message that the United States and China had a "common interest" in dealing with the Soviet Union. Therefore each could be "useful" to the other, despite many conflicting views.

Looking Forward also includes informative snapshots of Kissinger, who came to Beijing twice on Bush's watch ("whenever he was center stage, the Secretary seemed to come alive, like a political candidate working a crowd back home"), and Vice Premier Deng Xiaoping (later to be the top man in China), an "incessant chain smoker and tea drinker . . . who projected himself as a grassroots rural man-of-the-people, a rough-hewn soldier" but with an ability "to balance toughness and affability" when talking to foreign leaders.

The major interest in Bush's recollection of his Chinese experiences lies in his picture of Mao Tse-tung, then eighty-one years old and so deteriorated physically that women attendants had to help him out of his chair. Pointing to his head, he told Kissinger and Bush (who never saw the chairman alone) that "this part works well." But he then tapped his legs: "These parts do not work well [and] I also have some trouble with my lungs. In a word, I am not well." Then, smiling, the old Communist leader summed up his plight: "I am a showcase for visitors."

Bush observed a small oxygen tank in the room where "the leader of the world's biggest Communist country" received his American visitors—and stunned them with the words: "I am going to heaven soon. I have already received an invitation from God."

The witty Kissinger rose even to this occasion, telling the chairman: "Don't accept it soon."

Mao was not too sick, however, to shock the patrician Bush with a barnyard expression meaning "a dog fart," or to characterize U.S.–Chinese relations in graphically blunt terms. Holding up a fist and the little finger of the other hand, but indicating the fist, he said, "You are this." And of the little finger, "We are that. You have the atomic bomb and we don't."*

The opportunity that the Bushes had expected from their venture into the Far East did not quite materialize in great diplomatic or political events, and with typical realpolitik Kissinger told Bush, the maestro of friendship, "It doesn't matter whether [the Chinese] like you or not." In George Bush's view of the world such indifference was unthinkable; "my purpose," he recalled in a statement of national and personal faith, "wasn't to win popularity contests . . . but to get to know the Chinese— and to get them to know Americans—at a personal level."

Kissinger does not appear to have been a personal favorite of the ambassador. A pair of almost offhand entries in the diary Bush kept while in China offer revealing glimpses. The secretary of state was often "brilliant," in contrast to "the irritating manner he has of handling people. His staff are scared to death of him. . . . People quake . . . and don't dare tell him when he's keeping them waiting." And Bush may well have thought that Kissinger was calculating his own future when the secretary seemed to be "prob-

*Since China in fact had atomic weapons, Bush interpreted this to mean that Mao knew the United States was militarily stronger than China.

ing to see what my [Bush's] political plans were. I told him I had no political plans." Nevertheless, "Kissinger made some reference to my running for President in 1980." An early bid for appointment in a Bush administration?[14]

If so, Kissinger's timing was off, since George Bush did not become president until 1989.*

In November 1975 Kissinger cabled Beijing that President Ford wanted Bush to return to Washington to become director of the CIA. Neither George nor Barbara Bush wanted the assignment. The Bushes liked China and felt that they were just beginning to be effective there. Then, too, taking over an agency "battered by a decade of hostile congressional investigations, exposés, and charges that ran from lawbreaking to simple incompetence," as Bush put it in *Looking Forward,* was a little too reminiscent of heading the RNC during the Watergate years. And in the current atmosphere, Senate confirmation of any CIA director would not be easy.

Becoming the chief U.S. spy might also damage whatever Bush had accomplished in improving relations with China; and since the directorship of the CIA was supposed to be (though it seldom was) a nonpolitical job, it might be a dead-end street for Bush's American political prospects. In fact, however, an arcane

---

*In 1980, at the Republican National Convention in Detroit, Kissinger sought to make Gerald Ford the vice presidential running mate on Ronald Reagan's ticket. Reagan, sensing that a "co-presidency" would result, instead chose George Bush, who became vice president. Kissinger was never asked to serve in either of the Reagan administrations or in the subsequent Bush administration of 1989–93.

Washington political maneuver—suspected at the time and still believed by many—may well have been unfolding in 1975 and 1976.

Nelson Rockefeller, pushed by Ford in order to protect Ford's right flank from the right-wing presidential candidacy of Ronald Reagan, had taken himself out of the vice presidential competition for 1976 (which Bush did not know when Kissinger's cable arrived.)[15] Might not Ford's best choice for a replacement be the popular (among Republicans) George Bush, former ambassador to the UN and to China, whom Ford had passed over in choosing Rockefeller as vice president? Furthermore, as a Texas Republican, Bush might also help hold that important state against Reagan and later carry it against the Democrats.

If, on the other hand, Bush became director of the CIA, he not only would be in a supposedly nonpolitical position but would inevitably be tainted by all the investigations of and charges against an agency Senator Frank Church of Idaho had called "a rogue elephant out of control." That would rule out Bush for the vice presidency in 1976 and perhaps for good, leaving second place on the Ford ticket for someone else.

Who might be behind such a scheme, and why? The popular suspect was not Kissinger but Donald H. Rumsfeld, a renowned political infighter, who was at that time leaving the post of White House chief of staff to become secretary of defense (from which office James Schlesinger was being dismissed). But why would Rumsfeld,* unless he wanted the vice presidency for himself,

---

*The same "Rummy" brought back to Washington by President George W. Bush in 2001 as secretary of defense.

want Bush ruled out? Other Republicans, too, might have had reasons for wanting Bush sidelined; but no real cause for this elliptical political maneuver—if that's actually what happened—has ever been established. Nor, in retrospect, does George Bush in 1975—out of elective politics since 1970, never very effective when in them—seem to have been a likely vice presidential choice for 1976.*

In any event the Chinese government received the news of Bush's new appointment agreeably enough; Mao even told President Ford, who arrived on a visit as Bush was preparing to leave, that "we hate to see him go." Bush himself claims that the "key words" in Kissinger's telegram had been "the President asks." Faithful to his code of public service and to his family creed, Bush reasoned that "as long as what he'd asked me to do wasn't illegal or immoral, and I felt I could handle the job, there was only one answer I could give."[16] He gave it, and he and Barbara soon left for the United States "with mixed feelings."

Their apprehensions had not been misplaced; the confirmation battle in the Senate was tough and sustained. The chief CIA investigator, Senator Church, labeled Bush "too political" for the job; other critics wondered how a former Republican national chairman could be nonpolitical or independent.† The agency it-

---

*Ford ultimately chose Senator Bob Dole of Kansas as his running mate in 1976—the same Dole who was replaced by George Bush at the Republican National Committee in 1973, and who would later twice contest the party's presidential nomination with Bush. The Ford-Dole ticket lost a close race to Jimmy Carter and Walter Mondale.

†Including my *Times* colleague Anthony Lewis. I wrote, however, that Bush's political experience might be an asset as the CIA tried to regain credibility.

self was under heavy fire, Gerald Ford's political honeymoon was long over, and partisan jockeying for the 1976 election was constant.

Before Bush finally won confirmation as director of central intelligence (DCI),* Ford had to issue a solemn statement that "I will not consider him as my vice presidential running mate in 1976." That did it—though the idea of a CIA director running on a national ticket seems a political oxymoron anyway—and the Senate gave its approval.[17]

Bush's brief term as DCI—January 1976 to January 1977—appears to have been as relatively uneventful as his service at the UN and in China had been. In his first six months he testified thirty times before Congress and met with numerous individual members; made twelve changes in the top sixteen CIA slots; thought he observed improved relations with Congress if not the press; cemented a solid relationship with Brent Scowcroft, Ford's national security adviser (and later his own); and wrote to an old friend in Denver that "this is the most interesting job I've ever had."[18]

He recalled in *Looking Forward* that his main efforts had been to keep the "intelligence community" out of policy making, as originally envisioned in the law that created the National Security Council and the CIA during the Truman administration. Bush also recounts his struggles with a critical press and Congress.

Generally defending the CIA while conceding some of its blunders and miscues, he dwells on only two "crises"—in Beirut

*The CIA director also has considerable authority over other U.S. intelligence operations, such as those carried on by the National Security Agency; the latter mostly have to do with communications.

in the summer of 1976, following the assassination of Ambassador Francis E. Meloy Jr. and two other members of the embassy staff; and the efforts of Attorney General Edward Levi in the last days of the Ford administration to obtain sensitive CIA documents reclaimed from a would-be "mole," Edwin G. Moore. Breaking his established pattern of "getting along" even with adversaries, Bush actually had a brief "blow up" with Levi, one of the most distinguished attorneys general of modern times.

All this ignores, however, perhaps Bush's most significant act as director of intelligence—the acceptance of Team B as essentially a monitor of the CIA's work. Team B was a group of supposedly nonpartisan authorities on national security, none of them government officials, chaired by Richard Pipes, an expatriate Russian and a Harvard historian of the Soviet Union. Team B was appointed to review CIA intelligence estimates, working from the same data as had the agency. Bush's predecessors as DCI, including William Colby, had resisted such "threat reappraisal"; but when pressed by the Foreign Intelligence Advisory Board, Bush agreed to it with a typically breezy notation on a memo: "Let her fly! O.K. GB."

Team B proceeded to dispute CIA threat analyses, which then were focused on the Soviet Union, on almost every point—recommending higher defense spending in order to "catch up" with what it insisted was growing, if not superior, Soviet military strength. Team B's report was leaked and became the founding document of the so-called Committee on the Present Danger (CPD), composed of prestigious Republican and Democratic hawks. The CPD drove home to the public during the Carter administration and the first Reagan administration the idea that a "window of vulnerability" existed, which the United States had to close or fall into second place militarily.

Team B and the CPD were egregiously wrong, as forthcoming events in Eastern Europe and the Soviet Union were to demonstrate. But the committee's credibility and the American public's fear of the supposed Communist superpower were so great that the Reagan administration—Reagan himself a willing listener—unleashed a wave of defense spending throughout the 1980s, most of it unnecessary (though widely and erroneously credited today with forcing the Soviet Union into collapse).[19] Team B's arguments also made a strong impression on George H. W. Bush—as would be suggested in his first presidential campaign in 1980.

During the 1976 campaign, as DCI, Bush had been required to give Ford's Democratic opponent, Governor Jimmy Carter of Georgia, official intelligence briefings. After the election he again had to brief President-elect Carter, whom he found aloof but intelligent, with "an index-card mind"—but also "a loner, suspicious of strangers and their motives," who during a long and sensitive briefing "registered no emotion of any kind, asked for little follow-up and frankly seemed a little impatient."

In what appears to have been a casual statement, Carter once predicted that by 1985 "George [would] be President." Like Kissinger in China he was off in his timing, since Bush did not enter the White House until 1989. Neither Carter nor Bush could have known in 1976 that the ambitious and still-young Republican actually would run for president four years later, in 1980—and follow in Jimmy Carter's footsteps by becoming a serious candidate after scoring an upset victory in the Iowa caucuses.[20]

CHAPTER THREE

AFTER GERALD FORD lost the presidential election to Jimmy Carter in 1976, numerous voices speculated in the press that, as a unity gesture and for the sake of continuity in a sensitive post, Carter might keep George Bush as CIA director. Well before the inauguration, I wrote an op-ed column in the *New York Times* deprecating that idea—how could a former Republican national chairman be a bipartisan unity appointee? Almost immediately I received a phone call from Jody Powell, who was to be the new president's press secretary. As was his wont, Powell didn't mince words: "We're not going to do that."

Months before, I'd written that Governor Carter, then a relatively unknown candidate, was sure to lose the Florida Democratic primary to George Wallace of Alabama. Powell had called me then, too, and said just as bluntly: "We're think we're going to win in Florida."

Carter did win in Florida and went on to be nominated and defeat an incumbent president. So I trusted Powell's information when he told me Bush would not be reappointed. I didn't know, however, and Powell didn't tell me, that Bush actually had offered to stay on as DCI in a Democratic administration, not least because he had come to like the agency and the job and wanted to help restore the CIA to the high public standing he thought it deserved.[1] Once his offer was rejected, he found he did not like being at loose ends in Houston and out of a government position for the first time since he'd won election to Congress in 1966.

How do I "stay alive?" Bush wrote to ask Bayless Manning at the Council on Foreign Relations in New York, describing himself as "blessed by having had fascinating government assignments" and admitting to retaining his interest in national politics. In similar vein he wrote to Alan Greenspan, who had been Ford's economic adviser (and whom in 1992 Bush was to reappoint as chairman of the Federal Reserve), Charlie Bartlett, and others of his myriad friends.[2] It was politically advantageous to return to the business world, so Bush took on various lucrative business opportunities, being careful as a former DCI to avoid politically awkward conflicts of interest. All the while, however, thoughts of the presidency apparently were germinating in Bush's mind; he organized a PAC, the Fund for Limited Government (FLG), with his Houston neighbor, James A. Baker III, as chairman, and gathered a number of politically knowledgeable friends at Kennebunkport—the FLG footing the bill—to discuss his future.

Bush looked with an increasingly jaundiced eye on the presidency of Jimmy Carter, whom he regarded as weak and unskilled in the ways of Washington—but he listened carefully when Baker explained that Carter, by winning early in 1976 in the Iowa caucuses, had shown the way for a candidate with little national support to gain the name recognition a presidential candidate needed. Besides, like Carter in 1975, Bush saw no one else in his party with a more legitimate claim than his to the White House. And he was not yet convinced that Ronald Reagan, the front-runner, who had lost the 1976 nomination to Ford by only a whisker, could win in 1980.

Bush liked to claim that his extensive record of impressive posts—in Congress, at the UN, at the RNC, in China, at the CIA—qualified him for the presidency. Actually there was less to this claim than met the eye, and Bob Dole was to observe cuttingly in 1988 that *his* long years in the Senate had given him a real record, "not a resume." This clearly implied that Bush's vaunted experience was the other way around—a résumé, not a record—and not much of a qualification for the White House. That was *after* Bush had served eight years in the vice presidency—as the choice of Ronald Reagan more than of the American people.

Before the vice presidency, the Bush résumé was particularly thin. Lots of Americans, after all, have put in four years in the House of Representatives without running for president on the strength of this relatively minor achievement—and in Bush's case his two terms had resulted from only one challenged election. Counting his two Texas Senate races, he had never defeated an incumbent officeholder—and had beaten only one opponent of any kind, in 1966. Bush's two years at the UN had been unmarked by major crises and undercut by Nixon and Kissinger's "opening to China," his own year in Beijing was virtually uneventful, his party chairmanship had been devoted almost entirely to the loyal defense of Richard Nixon, and his labors at the CIA had been largely in sheltering the agency from the public, the press, and Congress. His two Senate campaigns had been competent but losers still; he had not won a competitive election since 1966 and that only in a congressional district all but tailored for him. All George Bush's most impressive-sounding jobs, in truth, had been appointive.

No standard of qualifications—save the age requirement of thirty-five and the U.S. residency requirement—exists for American-born presidential candidates of either party; but Bush's claim clearly was exaggerated—compared with, say, Dwight Eisenhower in 1952: no election experience at all but commander of Allied forces in Europe in World War II, army chief of staff, president of Columbia University, the first SACEUR (postwar supreme commander of NATO in Europe), leader in any number of national popularity and presidential preference polls.

Nevertheless Bob Dole's claim to superiority also lacked ultimate validity. A veteran senator does have a *voting* record on many issues, but that is not necessarily a political asset; he or she has little experience outside the Senate chamber, with other nations in world affairs, or with large-scale administration, hence little substantial experience for the presidency—witness the fact that in the twentieth century only two senators, Warren G. Harding and John F. Kennedy, have been elected directly from the Senate to the White House. In fact ten twentieth-century presidents—the two Roosevelts, Taft, Wilson, Coolidge, Hoover, Eisenhower, Carter, Reagan, and Clinton—never served in Congress at all.

Bush's variety of service, though he exaggerated the importance of each of his posts, actually gave him even in 1980 the kind of wide-ranging background experience that few senators achieve. He knew, or at least had met, political leaders around the world; he had dealt—though not very officially—with such great leaders as Mao Tse-tung. Like Dole, many in the press (including me) scoffed at Bush's claims for his résumé, but in the late 1970s it put him in demand to comment on major international issues, to make speeches for big and little causes and at rallies for local candidates.

All those friends listed in the card index Barbara Bush zealously maintained also were a major asset—school friends, political friends, business friends, family friends, money friends, and Republican activists in every state, some of whom were politically indebted to him. And in those days, as always, George Bush was never too tired to respond to political duty—which also was opportunity. As he began seriously to reach for the presidency, a major result was more cards in Barbara's growing index, more "due bills" owed him by other politicians. After every appearance he sent off notes to everyone he'd met who had helped him, who maybe someday *could* help him, even if they were then signed on with some other candidate. He took lessons from a speech coach (without much effect), shook thousands of hands, kissed babies tirelessly, ate plate after plate of banquet chicken and roamed the country from end to end—nearly two hundred thousand miles in one year. In these campaign travels he was accompanied only by David Bates, a young Houston lawyer who provided Bush's on-the-road staff (in 1978 Jim Baker was tied up running unsuccessfully for attorney general of Texas).

On May 1, 1979, two years after winding up his CIA service, George H. W. Bush announced that he was formally what he had been informally since leaving public service: a candidate for the Republican presidential nomination in 1980. In retrospect it may appear that he was overstepping himself; to some it did then; but his decision to run was no more brash—perhaps less so—than his effort in 1974, with a less impressive résumé, to persuade Gerald Ford to appoint him vice president. Every aspiring politician, at some point—or perhaps several—must risk the possibility that his reach will exceed his grasp.

Still following Carter's example, moreover, Bush and Baker focused on Iowa, organizing all ninety-nine of its counties, appearing in all of them time and again, working every gathering they could find, from lodge meetings to church barbecues. Bush was at his best in someone's living room before a dozen voters or in a town hall before fifty—and those, as Carter had shown, were the venues where the Iowa caucuses ultimately were won. Nor did Bush let his weak poll numbers—6 percent to Ronald Reagan's 45 in early January 1980—discourage him. He did not claim to be, or campaign as, a rigid conservative or a fierce liberal; let people think of him as they saw him, he reasoned—plain, friendly George Bush, who believed that his personal quality was more important to voters than any ideology or any political promise. And sure enough the gap slowly began to close; later in January the polls stood at Reagan, 33 percent; Bush, 27.

So it was that on the cold February night of the Iowa caucuses, George H. W. Bush defeated Reagan (who'd never even bothered to come to the state) by just over two thousand votes, or 1 percentage point: Bush, 30.5; Reagan, 29.4. And the Carter example held. By winning Bush got the bounce he needed into public recognition as a serious candidate, plus the inflow of campaign funds that resulted, even a cover story and photo in *Newsweek.* Now he had "Big Mo"—lots of momentum—the upbeat candidate exulted. If so, it had come just in time for the New Hampshire primary, which now could be pictured as what the Bush campaign had long wanted: a one-on-one showdown with Ronald Reagan.

Perhaps it was inexperience in presidential campaigning, or maybe the effect of their belief in Big Mo. Neither George Bush nor his aides took seriously enough the plain fact that Reagan had come within a percentage point of winning in Iowa—without campaigning or appearing in the state.

More than one candidate in more than one race has come to regret a longed-for showdown with the Great Communicator—Edmund G. Brown in California in 1966, for instance, or Jimmy Carter and Walter Mondale in the presidential debates of 1980 and 1984. I well remember attending a luncheon with Vice President Mondale at the *New York Times* just after the Democratic National Convention at Madison Square Garden had renominated him and Carter in 1980. Mondale was supremely confident about the impending campaign against Reagan, even suggesting it would be "like Goldwater again."

Earlier that year the Reagan campaign, stung by its candidate's narrow loss in Iowa and by Bush's risky claim to Big Mo, approached Bush's New Hampshire chairman, former Governor Hugh Gregg,* with the idea of a Reagan-Bush televised debate.[3] Gregg and Bush accepted the idea, since it emphasized their contention that Iowa had made the Republican nomination contest a two-man race. In fact, however, there were four other candidates: Representative John Anderson of Illinois, Senator Bob Dole of Kansas, Senator Howard Baker of Tennessee, and Representative Phil Crane of Illinois, an aggressive conservative.

A debate sponsor was found in the *Nashua Telegraph* and a moderator in its editor, Jon Breen. The event was scheduled for

*Bush was as well organized in New Hampshire in 1980 as he had been in Iowa. Twenty years later, Bush's son, George W., called on some of those who had worked for his father to help with *his* New Hampshire primary campaign against Senator John McCain.

Saturday night, February 23, at the Nashua High School. But the Federal Elections Commission ruled that if a newspaper was to sponsor the debate, *all* candidates would have to be included. So Reagan's New Hampshire organization decided to pick up the cost of the debate and hold it to the originally scheduled two-candidate clash. But hours before the debate was to begin, Bush's press spokesman, Pete Teeley, picked up rumors that John Sears, then Reagan's campaign manager, was inviting the other four candidates to show up at the high school that night.*

Bush's attitude was that it was too late to change the rules set by the *Telegraph* even though the newspaper was no longer the debate sponsor. But when he, James Baker (who was not related to Howard Baker of Tennessee), and another aide, David Keene, reached their readying room for the debate, Sears came in to say he thought it would be a good idea to open the debate to all candidates. Jim Baker and Keene immediately demurred—the audience was there to see Reagan versus Bush, they said, not another candidate "cattle show." Bush himself added the objection that the *Telegraph*'s original ground rules should not be broken.

When Jon Breen, Bush, and Reagan appeared onstage, however, Anderson, Dole, Howard Baker, and Crane came right behind them, and stood there stolidly—and rather comically—abreast, obviously having no intention of leaving voluntarily. Breen stubbornly refused audience calls to expand the debate to include the four. Behind the scenes Bush already had rejected a party-unity plea from Senator Gordon Humphrey, Republican

---

*The idea actually was inspired by the resourceful Bob Dole, who resented being left out of the debate and also resented George Bush, dating back to their Waldorf-Astoria meeting in 1970.

of New Hampshire. But Reagan, speaking into the microphone in front of him, began a speech saying that everyone should be included—whereupon Jon Breen, obviously a more aggressive moderator than most, ordered Reagan's microphone shut off.

Reagan replied loudly and briskly, with a characteristic malapropism and a quote from an old movie.*

"I *paid* for this microphone, Mr. Green!"

The crowd—including the four excluded candidates—cheered and applauded. Reagan, handsome and genial, stood to shake the hand of each of the four as they straggled off the stage, apparently mollified or at least persuaded to leave, to hold a news conference of their own elsewhere in the building. Reagan's instinctive reply—from his extensive movie memory—had provided one of the great moments of the 1980 campaign, one that not only stamped out Big Mo but finished, for all practical purposes, the first presidential campaign of George Bush—who through it all had just sat there, silent and unmoving, as if he knew neither what to say nor what to do.

At the impromptu news conference of the other candidates, Dole pronounced bitter but—as it ultimately turned out—premature judgment: "As far as George Bush is concerned, he'd better find himself another party."

The ensuing debate, like most, has been deservedly forgotten. But afterward the Nashua school parking lot was littered with discarded BUSH FOR PRESIDENT signs. Reagan put in two more days of campaigning before the primary vote on Tuesday, but George Bush went home to Houston—not exactly with his

---

State of the Union (1948), starring Spencer Tracy and Katharine Hepburn.

tail between his legs but no doubt anticipating what he was about to get: a sound defeat. Reagan 50 percent, Bush 23, all others trailing, made it a two-man race, all right—just not the one Bush and Jim Baker had wanted.

Bush plowed on bravely: "I was—and am—an optimist, convinced that no matter how bad a situation might look, something good can come of it. It's ingrained, part of my nature."[4] He even won a few important primaries—Massachusetts, Michigan, Connecticut, Pennsylvania. In the last of these states, perhaps unfortunately, he or a speechwriter coined the immortal phrase "voodoo economics," to describe Reagan's program of tax cuts combined with increases in military spending.

On at least one occasion Bush also appeared susceptible to the arguments of the so-called Team B that, as DCI, he had allowed to review CIA threat appraisals. While flying from Houston to New Orleans in a chartered jet in January 1980, he was interviewed by the lone reporter accompanying him, Robert Scheer of the *Los Angeles Times*. Bush criticized President Carter for not pushing ahead with the MX missile and the B-1 bomber—echoing a point made by Team B and frequently voiced by the CPD and by Ronald Reagan. Scheer observed that these weapons could make little difference in a nuclear war.

"Not if you believe nuclear war can't be won," Bush replied. "I don't believe that." He then went on to explain *how* a nuclear war could be won: "You have a survivability of command and control, survivability of industrial potential, protection of a percentage of your citizens, and you have the capability that inflicts more damage on the opposition than it can inflict upon you. That's the way you can have a winner."

Then he quickly added: "The Soviet Union's planning is based on the ugly concept of winning a nuclear exchange."

"Do you mean five percent could survive," Scheer asked. "Two percent?"

"More than that," Bush insisted. "If everybody fired everything they've got, you'd have more than that survive."

After Scheer published these remarks in the *Los Angeles Times,* Bush and his aides, when questioned, would point to that last sentence about "Soviet . . . planning." Bush had not been expressing his own views, they insisted, but describing Soviet attitudes.[5] Maybe so, but Bush's words almost exactly predicted the "war-fighting" and civil defense talk of the first Reagan administration, in which Bush was to become a loyal vice president. Reagan himself did not become convinced until later of his famous formulation: "A nuclear war cannot be won and must never be fought."

The same night Bush won the primary in Michigan, Reagan picked up enough delegates in Nebraska to make his nomination certain. So, ten days later, at a Houston news conference on May 30, 1980, Bush finally gave in to the facts and announced that his campaign was at an end—an unhappy moment for even a confirmed optimist. His political future was in doubt, and soon he even reawakened the persistent question about his identity, selling his Houston house and buying the big Walker's Point family property in Kennebunkport. Was he a real Texan or a New England carpetbagger?*

It might have been better politics to let the Maine estate re-

---

*A biographer, Herbert Parmet, tried to solve the problem by calling Bush a "Lone Star Yankee."

vert to what it had been before the Walker family bought it—
Damon Park, a spit of land jutting into the Atlantic and for years
a favorite outing spot for Kennebunkport townspeople (though
maybe not all the way back to Revolutionary times, when the
town was known as Arundel). But George Bush had spent his
summers while growing up and many later ones at Walker's
Point; Uncle Herbert Walker, who had inherited the place from
his father, old George H. Walker, had died, and Herbert's sons
wanted George H. W. Bush, the family star and favorite, to take
over. Besides, the alternative was not reversion of Walker's Point
to a public park, however that might have diminished the "elitist" charge that clung to the failed presidential candidate. A group
of Arab investors wanted to buy the estate, break it up, and par-
cel out the attractive land. In the end it was a family matter: Herbert Walker's widow, Mary, sold the Point to her nephew George
Bush for less than the Arabs offered.[6]

So, in addition to being out of politics and out of Texas, Bush
had gone into debt. He did have some faint hope, however, as
anyone must have who holds the second hand in a presidential
campaign, of being chosen as Reagan's running mate. Officially
a Texas Republican who could not only help carry that state
(third largest in the Union) but also supply the foreign-policy
experience Reagan lacked, a candidate who had won other important states in the primary contest, a supposed moderate to
balance Reagan's conservatism, Bush might be a strong vice presidential candidate and even a sort of party-unity choice.

He did not know, however, that largely owing to the Nashua
debate debacle in New Hampshire—and probably to his "voodoo economics" remark—not only Bob Dole but Ronald Reagan
himself was unfavorably impressed. Reagan thought Bush was

too easily rattled by criticism and might not be tough enough to be president, hence should not be even the proverbial "heartbeat away."

At first nothing at the 1980 Detroit convention gave Bush any more than the small hope raised by his primary campaign. In fact it appeared that Reagan might even fall for a scheme being pushed by the still-ambitious Henry Kissinger—aching for a comeback after four years of wandering in the political wilderness during a Democratic administration. Kissinger nearly sold Reagan on the remarkable notion that with Reagan's old rival of 1976, former president Gerald Ford, he could form an unbeatable "dream ticket." Ford was agreeable, provided he had a "meaningful role" as vice president in the new Republican administration, and Kissinger could all but taste a new term in power.

Ford himself blew up this pipe dream. In a television interview with Walter Cronkite, he was pressed to explain what he considered a meaningful role and replied so confidently that George Bush, watching, was sure the deal must be all set. But Ronald Reagan was watching, too, apparently with a growing feeling that he was being had—an attitude no doubt shared by his wife, Nancy, always alert to any threat to the fortunes of her adored "Ronnie."

"This is really two presidents [Ford is] talking about," Reagan later recalled thinking as he watched. Later that night he met Ford behind closed hotel-room doors. Predictably, when their meeting ended, the "dream ticket" and Kissinger's ambitions lay on the floor in tatters.

"[Ford] didn't think it was right for him or for me. And now I'm inclined to agree," Reagan explained to his staff. Wanting to settle the running-mate question quickly, however, he immediately put in a call to another possibility.

"I'm calling George Bush . . . anybody have an objection?"[7]

Nobody did—including, of course, a surprised Bush, who'd already retired for the night. Later, at the door of their hotel room, in bathrobes, he and Barbara talked with television reporters about the surprising new prospect before them. Once again George Bush was moving up—on the patronage of still another president.*

They could hardly have lost. Reagan—the Gipper of movie fame,[†] the so-called Great Communicator of contemporary politics— was the nation's most charismatic conservative (though "an amiable dunce," in the opinion of the veteran Democratic sage Clark Clifford). President Carter was unpopular, unable to bring home the American hostages then being held in Iran, and too often politically unwise—he had appeared personally on television, for instance, to announce the bloody failure of a helicopter-borne attempt to rescue the hostages. Unemployment was over 7 percent, inflation had risen to 13 percent, and as a consequence the Federal Reserve had pegged the prime interest rate at 15.

Under all those conditions it was not surprising that the Reagan-Bush ticket was a big winner—489 electoral votes to 49

*His third. After the Reagan-Bush ticket won the election of 1980, George Bush became vice president of the United States on January 20, 1981.

†In his Hollywood days, Reagan had played the Notre Dame football star George Gipp, in the movie *Knute Rockne, All-American*. After Gipp's death in 1925 from a throat infection, Rockne tried to inspire a losing 1928 team, as the movie had it, by exclaiming, "Win one for the Gipper!"

for Carter-Mondale. Reagan had turned out to be no Goldwater; his coattails also carried in a Republican Senate, the first since 1955, although the Democrats managed to keep control of the House.* Probably nothing running mate Bush could have done, short of causing some kind of national scandal, could have brought about defeat; but his efforts did not add much to the victory either. Bush's major contribution was his mere presence at Reagan's side, which no doubt soothed the wounds of those elderly party members who remembered—who were, in fact, the remnants of—Eisenhower's and Prescott Bush's "modern Republican" faction in the fifties.

A vice president, no matter where his office may be located or how his efforts may be extolled by the president and hyped by associates, has rarely had much influence on policy or much power in any administration. Nixon under Eisenhower was perhaps the first vice president even to appear to be important; he tried to picture himself as a sort of "assistant president" but even to him and his successors, the jobs assigned—jetting to notable funerals abroad, heading well-named committees or commissions ("reinventing government"), attending and often speaking at routine party functions—were mostly just that: assigned jobs, different only in prestige and prominence from the assigned jobs of White House assistants and other bureaucrats.

A vice president's constitutional functions consist of (a) presiding over the Senate (though he actually wields the gavel infre-

*They kept it throughout Reagan's two terms and won back the Senate in 1986.

quently, usually only when he may have to break a tie vote), and (b) succeeding to office if the president dies—though this function was merely assumed and not specified in the Constitution until the Twenty-fifth Amendment was ratified in 1967—or taking on its powers and duties while a president declares himself disabled (which has never happened). Most vice presidents, therefore, have been mere ciphers, holding office only because presidential nominees tapped them for the ticket, usually for political reasons. Eisenhower even allowed a committee of Republican eminences to choose Nixon for his running mate; FDR, in his four terms, actually had three different vice presidents— John Nance Garner, Henry Wallace, and Harry Truman. The last of these was so far out of the game in 1945, when he took office after Roosevelt died, that he knew nothing about the Manhattan Project or the development of the atomic bomb.

Bush was no great exception to the rule, although he benefited from the fact that Carter had given Mondale, Bush's predecessor as vice president, a White House office and more prominence and access than most "veeps" had had; so Reagan at least pretended to do as much as Carter had done. Bush, moreover, exerted all his considerable gifts for making friends to recommend himself to Reagan; his lifelong devotion to loyalty and team play— and his own continuing ambition—made it natural for him to avoid criticizing the president or differing with him in any significant way.

Their contrasting political attitudes he managed to accept as easily as he had cast his lot with Barry Goldwater in 1964, or turned from past criticism of the UN to enthusiasm for it in 1970. Bush sternly insisted to the vice presidential staff that there should be no "leaks," and there were none. And as he had understood in his UN years that he was an "advocate," not a policy maker, he now saw that he could not be and should not try to be a decision maker in the Reagan administration.

Bush was determined, however, to win the president's personal trust and friendship; that was not only his nature, it was also a political necessity. If he ever hoped to have the confidence and backing of the conservatives who idolized Reagan and had come to dominate the Republican Party, it would not be enough to "talk the talk" as a mere Texas oilman; he would have to "walk the walk" as a solid conservative; that would require a rightward conversion like that of his 1964 Senate campaign.

Bush never hesitated. A week after the election, he sent off a courteous, not-quite-obsequious note to the new president: "Thanks for making us feel so welcome, thanks for the joy of working with you, thanks for those little touches of grace and humor and affection that make life sing. . . . I will never do anything to embarrass you politically."[8]

He didn't. Before long, he was being met more or less halfway by the Gipper himself—an amiable Irishman liked by almost everyone who met him, including another, very different amiable Irishman, Thomas P. "Tip" O'Neill of Massachusetts, who became the Democratic Speaker of the House. This typified Reagan's instinct which—Bush recalled in *Looking Forward*—was "to think the best of the people he works with."[9]

Reagan not only assigned him Mondale's former White House office but adopted the Carter policy of granting his vice president complete and open access to the Oval Office. Soon, too, the former Republican rivals were having lunch, completely alone, each Thursday—with the understanding, always observed, that no topic was forbidden but that everything said would remain between them. The occasion usually catered to their shared taste for Mexican food, and to Reagan's appetite for jokes*—so much so that Bush browbeat his staff into providing him with a new joke for each luncheon. He was often able, moreover, to bring back a Reagan joke, sometimes two, to the vice presidential staff.

The emerging relationship profited also from the president's appointment of Bush's close friend, the wily James Baker III, as White House chief of staff. During the primaries Baker's skills and intelligence in managing the Bush campaign had impressed Reagan, the press, and everybody else. After Bush was forced to end his candidacy, Baker took over the Reagan campaign, then the new White House staff—all without sacrificing his long friendship with Bush. Baker's leading role in the administration kept Bush well informed, on the one hand, and helped to mollify any resentments, on the other, that might have arisen among longtime Reagan aides.

Bush finally achieved something like the relationship that he sought with Reagan after the president was nearly fatally wounded outside the Washington Hilton Hotel on March 30, 1981, just over two months after being sworn in.

At the time Vice President Bush had just spoken at a ceremony in Fort Worth, Texas, celebrating the designation as a national landmark of the Old Hotel Texas—coincidentally where President Kennedy had spent the last night of his life on November 21, 1963.

---

*A friend of mine once was afforded a tour of the private quarters in the White House and discovered that the book on Reagan's bedside table was entitled *Five Hundred Irish Jokes.*

As *Air Force 2,* the vice presidential plane, was taking off for Austin, where Bush was to speak to the Texas legislature, Ed Pollard, the chief of his Secret Service detail, reported grim news from Washington. An attempt had been made on Reagan's life, and two agents "were down." Secretary of State Al Haig then called the plane to advise Bush to return to Washington; so did Secretary of the Treasury Donald Regan. A coded message disclosed that the president had been shot and was undergoing surgery at George Washington University Hospital.

At Austin, Bush decided to scrub his schedule in the state capital, *Air Force 2* refueled, and the vice president called Washington for more information. Then the great plane took off, flying northeast, Bush refusing to talk with the onboard press until he knew more about what had happened.

On the descent into Andrews Air Force Base outside Washington, Pollard and a military aide advised Bush to take a helicopter directly to the White House for a scheduled meeting with the cabinet and the National Security Council. It would take much longer, they said, to fly as usual to the landing pad at the Naval Observatory, the vice presidential residence, then drive to the White House through late-afternoon traffic. And by going direct they'd reach the White House in time to make the 7 P.M. television news and reassure an anxious country.

Bush knew by then, via a message from Ed Meese, Reagan's close associate, that the president had survived the surgery and was recovering. With that in mind the vice president refused the suggestion that he be helicoptered straight to the White House. His explanation, as he recalls it in *Looking Forward,* was a classic statement of traditional vice presidential deference—and of

George Bush's personal credo of loyalty and team play: "Only the President lands on the south lawn."[10]

Bush's performance in this crisis, the first of the new administration, impressed Reagan. The two men never became close in a warm, personal way, but the distant, rather unengaged Reagan, despite his joviality, had few such relationships outside his marriage to Nancy—not even with his children. But Bush kept his access privileges, attended those Thursday luncheons faithfully, kept digging up new jokes, and carried out a vice president's accustomed official and political functions. So far as is known, Bush was never out of favor or treated as an "outsider"—except briefly in Reagan's second term, when for the vice president's own political purposes he claimed to have been "out of the loop" and unaware of the administration's Iran-Contra maneuverings.

On the other hand, try as he might, and despite his fervent fealty to Ronald Reagan, Bush never could quite dispel the suspicions of Republican conservatives that he was, in fact, an eastern internationalist with moderate tendencies and elitist attitudes— and was therefore neither sincere nor wholly reliable. The columnist and commentator George Will, a Reagan fan, labeled the vice president a "lap dog" for his dogged efforts to win conservative support. Bush had even tried to make friends with the most conservative publisher in the nation, New Hampshire's redoubtable William Loeb of the *Manchester Union-Leader,* and had worked relentlessly to persuade conservatives John Sununu and John Ashcroft that he was genuinely opposed to abortion—not easy with Barbara Bush looking over his shoulder. Will's epithet was only an extreme example of the—not altogether misplaced—

conservative reservations that followed Bush throughout the Reagan years and into his own presidential term.

In these circumstances Bush fell naturally into the early attitude of the Reagan administration that a nuclear war could be fought and won—an attitude epitomized when Reagan signed a National Security Decision Document in 1982, committing the nation to fight and win such a war. His security adviser, Richard Pipes, expressing the general view of Team B, declared that "the probability of nuclear war is 40 percent . . . and our strategy is winnable nuclear war."[11]

Falling in with this general atmosphere of the administration may or may not have earned Bush points from the conservatives surrounding him. It hardly disturbed the vice presidential good life. From the official residence at the Naval Observatory on Massachusetts Avenue, the Bushes plunged into an active social life, traveling a great deal around the country and overseas, enjoying themselves but also working hard at making friends for the administration, the president, and the future of George Bush. He kept a voting residence in Houston, at the Houstonian Hotel, attended fund-raisers and made appearances or speeches or both anywhere he might help some good Republican get elected. He became adept at throwing out the first ball at baseball games,* and never failed to thank the motorcycle cops who cleared the way for his limousine. *Air Force 2* was perhaps his greatest asset—local leaders and candidates were overjoyed to be

*After one of which, the N.Y. Mets versus the St. Louis Cardinals on opening day 1985, Bush wrote to Nelson Doubleday, an owner of the Mets, that the event had given him a thrill "right up there with seeing Joan Williams naked when I was 8." Bush, *All the Best*, p. 345.

invited for a ride with the vice president, to talk politics or sports with him, down a martini, make friends. George Bush made friends wherever he went, as he always had—so many of them that when he first ran for president in 1980 and was asked why he thought he could win, he had answered in all seriousness: "I've got a big family and lots of friends."[12]

As vice president, he still sent out notes in a steady stream of thanks and good fellowship, all those addresses going into the ever-expanding card index. And though television comics might wisecrack about the many funerals of foreign leaders at which he represented the United States, he knew those funerals were opportunities to get further acquainted abroad, make himself personally known to those he hoped someday to work with, and add friends overseas to all those at home.

In 1982, for example, he traveled on official business to Asia, went to the funeral of King Khalid in Saudi Arabia, attended the inauguration of President Belisario Betancur in Colombia, and started on a trip to Africa, before being dispatched to Moscow for the funeral of Leonid Brezhnev—"a funeral without God," Bush reported to Reagan. In Moscow he rubbed elbows with such leaders as President Zia ul-Haq of Pakistan, Prime Minister Ichiro Suzuki of Japan, and many others. He chatted with Yuri Andropov, Brezhnev's successor, about the days when Andropov had headed the KGB and Bush the CIA. Then the vice president and his wife resumed their interrupted African trip—a learning experience about that continent's "economic crisis."[13]

Some of his overseas trips had important purposes other than funeral observances. In February 1983, for instance, Bush braved angry and insulting demonstrators in London to defend U.S. deployment of intermediate-range missiles in Europe. The

Soviets already had such missiles in place, threatening European cities and the half-million American troops then assigned to the Continent. Bush's speech in London helped counter popular objections to a deployment European governments actually had requested.[14]

At home Bush focused on two rather typical vice presidential chores. He headed a special government task force on "regulatory relief"—in plain English, a commission to study the maze of rules and regulations previously established by the federal government and to determine which might be eliminated or needed revision; and he chaired another group pondering the problem of international drug smuggling, particularly the flow of illegal drugs into the United States. Unhappily both subjects were later to bob up on his presidential desk, in the "savings and loan crisis" that greeted his administration, and in the brief war on Panama that resulted in the capture of the demagogue and drug smuggler Manuel Antonio Noriega (an arm's-length associate from Bush's CIA days).

Noriega was the cause of one recorded exception to the vice president's customary humility. In 1988 the Reagan Justice Department indicted the Panamanian dictator for drug trafficking and racketeering, but there seemed to be no way to bring him to trial in the United States. Secretary of State Shultz proposed that both the indictment and some sanctions that had been imposed on Panama should be lifted—if Noriega would get out of Panama and stay out.

When Gen. Colin Powell, then Reagan's national security adviser, briefed Bush on Shultz's idea, Bush said he had "no problem" with it. But a conversation with Daryl Gates, the hard-line chief of Los Angeles police, convinced the vice president that

dismissing the indictment would be a betrayal of all the law en-
forcement officers who had died in the battle against drugs.

Then, Powell recalled, "Bush did something none of us had
ever seen him do before. He argued with the President directly in
front of the rest of us. The deal was bad, bad, bad and the President should not go through with it."

Reagan, however, was "immovable." He went ahead with the
plan—which was promptly spurned by Noriega. All negotiations of that kind collapsed, and the dictator remained in
place.[15]

Earlier, as the election year 1984 approached, Bush had so
consolidated his position with Reagan that, even from suspicious conservatives, no serious threat arose that he might be
"dumped"—though vice presidents have often been the most
expendable of officials. Nor was the campaign itself in much
doubt; Reagan was regarded as a sure bet to be reelected over the
Democratic presidential nominee, Walter Mondale, and Bush
would be returned along with him. Nevertheless it was a difficult campaign for the vice president, owing to Mondale's unprecedented choice of a running mate—Representative Geraldine
Ferraro of New York, the first woman ever to be named on a national ticket.

That was difficult in itself, as Ferraro was the choice of many
women and not a few men, for sentimental if not political reasons. But she and her husband, a real estate executive, suffered
criticism in the press for tax entanglements; and Bush resented
the fact that reporters then began to search *his* tax records, without finding anything culpable. Barbara Bush was angered by
comparisons of Bush with Ferraro, in which he was referred to as
an "elitist," while she was often supposed to be a sort of blue-

collar candidate. Actually Ferraro and her husband were wealthy, and once Mrs. Bush incautiously denounced "that four-million-dollar ———— I can't say it but it rhymes with rich." She later apologized, but the remark made headlines and further complicated Bush's campaign.

The worst happened, however, after the only Bush-Ferraro debate. The next day, the vice president was quoted as saying that he had tried "to kick a little ass last night." Bush later explained that he had not known his words were being picked up by a boom mike, and that, anyway, he was only repeating the slogan on a sign being carried by some longshoremen with whom he was meeting in New Jersey. Even if that was so, the explanation came too late to forestall the predictable criticism.[16]

Nothing, however, could stop Reagan's all but inevitable re-election,* which meant that in January 1985, George Bush entered his second term as vice president and Ronald Reagan his last in the White House. Even as they took their oaths and watched the inaugural parade, talk and preparations began for the politics of far-off 1988 and Bush's continuing presidential ambition.

*Mondale and Ferraro failed even to carry his home state of Minnesota. The electoral count was 525 to 13.

CHAPTER FOUR

IN JULY 1979 the Nicaraguan dictatorship of Anastasio Somoza collapsed. A broad revolutionary coalition, the Sandinista* National Liberation Front, took power in Nicaragua, and was at first welcomed by the Carter Administration in Washington. The coalition soon split, however, and the leftist Daniel Ortega emerged as its leader. The Sandinista government then extended arms aid to a leftist guerrilla movement in El Salvador, accepted economic, scientific, and cultural assistance from the Soviet Union, and welcomed Cuban "advisers."

When the fiercely anti-Communist Ronald Reagan came to the U.S. presidency in 1981, he quickly canceled all aid to Nicaragua and instituted a "covert action" program, ostensibly to stop the flow of arms into El Salvador, but with the larger objective of keeping Central America out of the Soviet-Cuban orbit. To the same ends the CIA also formed ties with the Nicaraguan Democratic Force, an anti-Sandinista organization based in Honduras; it included many former Somoza followers, and its fighting forces were familiarly known as "the contras." By 1982 the Reagan administration, through the CIA, was backing the contras with arms and money, despite considerable public and congressional support for the Sandinistas.

*Named for an earlier Nicaraguan revolutionary, Augusto Cesar Sandino.

Tom Wicker

A congressional amendment sponsored by Representative
Edward P. Boland, Democrat of Massachusetts, was intended to
cut off all U.S. financial support for the overthrow of the
Nicaraguan government. To evade this prohibition Reagan
signed a "finding" stating that the purpose of aid to the contras
was only to interdict the flow of arms into El Salvador. But in
1984 the CIA, with Reagan's approval, mined three Nicaraguan
harbors, hoping to disrupt shipping into and out of the country.
The agency neglected to inform Congress in advance, as required by law, and news of the mining caused a public outcry.

Barry Goldwater, Republican of Arizona and chairman of the
Senate Intelligence Committee, protested to the CIA; and Senator
Daniel P. Moynihan, Democrat of New York, resigned from the
committee (though he later rejoined it). A second, stronger
Boland Amendment was passed, this one prohibiting the use of
appropriated funds for "military or paramilitary operations in
Nicaragua by any nation, group, organization, movement or in-
dividual," particularly including any "agency or entity of the
United States *involved in intelligence activities* [italics added]."

The Reagan administration nevertheless had committed itself, at all costs, to holding the contras together. And Boland II,
as it was known, would be effective for only one year, until December 1985. It might possibly be defeated after that, and for the
intervening twelve months might be evaded in one of two ways:
by working through the NSC staff* instead of the CIA, on the

*Actually, though the NSC is not authorized to participate in covert
activities, Lt. Col. Oliver North of the NSC staff already had been involved in the mining of the Nicaraguan harbors. North was to work
closely with Director William Casey of the CIA in continuing administration support of the contras.

pretext that the NSC was not an entity "involved in intelligence activities," or by using private or third-nation funds instead of money appropriated by Congress.

In a different policy for a different part of the world, the Reagan administration also, by 1983, was loudly and insistently committed to Operation Staunch—an international campaign designed to punish the Iranian regime of the Ayatollah Ruholla Khomeini by denying it the purchase of arms. After the ouster of the shah, Iran was accused of supporting terrorism and fostering Islamic fundamentalism; but its worst offense—in Washington's view—was to have held Americans hostage during the Carter administration.

Operation Staunch tolerated no deals with terrorists, no bargaining for the release of hostages, no compromise with blackmail. That policy clearly applied to seven Americans who had been taken hostage and were being held in Lebanon by groups believed in Washington to be pro-Iranian or even controlled from Tehran. Even so, some elements of the Reagan administration had expressed interest in improving relations with Iran *after* the death of the ayatollah; but a National Security Council study of that prospect came to nothing. At the end of 1984, with Reagan reelected, Operation Staunch remained the official U.S. policy toward Iran.

In November of that year, however, a former CIA official named Theodore Shackley had met in Hamburg, Germany, with several Iranians, including Manucher Ghorbanifar, an international trader and mystery man known unfavorably to the CIA. At this meeting Ghorbanifar worried openly that Iran eventually might be overwhelmed by the Soviet Union, a prospect sure to engage Washington's interest. He also suggested that a "moderate" political faction existed in Tehran, raised the possibility of the United States' selling TOW* missiles to these moderates, and even talked of a cash ransom for the release of four of the American hostages being held in Lebanon. Ghorbanifar of course offered himself as a middleman to pursue these possibilities.

Shackley, who had no official status, scoffed at the idea of missile sales but nevertheless informed the State Department of the Hamburg meeting. His memo evoked no real response, and Ghorbanifar could stimulate no further action until he met with the legendary Saudi Arabian millionaire and businessman Adnan Kashoggi, probably in April 1985. Kashoggi heard him out, as one huckster to another, and saw the possibility of an international statesman's role for himself—an idea congenial even to a man with a forty-million-dollar DC-8 and twelve Mercedes limousines. He checked on Ghorbanifar with the Israelis; they vouched for him, whereupon a number of meetings of Americans, Israelis, and Iranians followed (the details of which are multitudinous, varied, and often conflicting). The net result was that even the tough-minded Israelis were "convince[d] . . . that they had an inside track into the hitherto secret world of Iranian politics and [were] persuaded . . . that they could profitably share their newfound knowledge with the Americans."[1]

It's unnecessary here to develop further the confusing details of how the Reagan administration, despite Operation Staunch, Boland II, and the Constitution, conceived what Oliver North of the NSC called a "neat" idea: secretly selling arms to Iran, with

*"Tube-launched, optically tracked, wire-guided" missiles.

the willing assistance of Israel, to pursue an improved "strategic relationship" and in the process free some American hostages—then secretly using part of the arms-sale profits to support the contra war against the Sandinistas.

It may be an overstatement, however, to suggest that the administration "conceived" that idea—or any idea at all. Rather, a "process" seems to have gone forward without official or proper "staffing" and to have been conducted mostly by men of no real authority, who did not necessarily know what others were doing, and who were motivated more to succeed than to observe the scruples of the law.

That's another story, replete with clandestine meetings, secret bank accounts, international intrigue, fortune, and folly. It was almost accidentally exposed in 1987, ruining both "covert" schemes and nearly causing Reagan's impeachment. But that involved story concerns George H. W. Bush primarily with regard to three questions: What did Reagan's vice president know about these operations, when did he know it, and what, if anything, did he do to bring the administration back to a more considered and lawful course? The answers are reasonably if not entirely clear:

What did he know? Quite a lot, as close study of the record suggests.

When did he know it? Soon enough to have lent weight to the opposition—and there *was* an opposition.

What did he do with this knowledge? Very little, so far as is known—but perhaps more than he or anyone else has disclosed.

On March 4, 1987, on television, President Reagan addressed an Iran-contra affair that already had been the subject of extensive congressional investigation, several other probes both private and official, and press accounts too numerous to list:

> A few months ago [Reagan said], I told the American people I did not trade arms for hostages. My heart and my best intentions still tell me that's true, but the facts and the evidence tell me it is not. What began as a strategic opening to Iran deteriorated, in its implementation, into trading arms for hostages.

As early as 1985, in fact, the Reagan administration had been in turmoil on precisely that question: whether efforts to work out a new strategic relationship with Iran could or should include the sale of arms.

In outspoken opposition was Secretary of State George Shultz, who vigorously pointed out the obvious: Such arms sales would violate the clear policy of the president himself and his administration—Operation Staunch. While urging other nations not to sell arms to Iran, how could the United States possibly make such sales itself, even in secret?

Also in unmistakable opposition—though on slightly different grounds from Shultz's—was Secretary of Defense Caspar "Cappy" Weinberger. He thought Iran an "irrational" nation and that it was "lunacy" to believe in "moderates" playing a significant role, or even existing, in it.

These two senior Cabinet members, those most involved in foreign and security policies, made a formidable opposition. But a more numerous faction believed that selling arms to Iran might help achieve a "diplomatic breakthrough." This group "presumably" included Robert McFarlane, the national security adviser; his assistant, Admiral John Poindexter; William Casey, director of the CIA; Oliver North of the NSC staff; Donald Regan, the White House chief of staff;* Vice President Bush; and "most important," Ronald Reagan himself.[2]

Logs of a White House meeting on August 6, 1985, indisputably record Bush's presence. At that meeting McFarlane announced that Iran wanted one hundred TOW missiles in exchange for four hostages; Shultz denounced what he termed "a very bad idea," and said "we [would be] just falling into the arms for hostages business, and we shouldn't do it." Weinberger also was outspoken in opposition.

Months later, on January 6, 1986, Bush again was present when Poindexter reported that the ante had been raised, briefing President Reagan on an Israeli scheme for exchanging four thousand TOWs for *all* the hostages. The next day, January 7, a meeting of the NSC was convened to discuss the issue further. Bush, as vice president a statutory NSC member, was among those present, of whom George Shultz later recalled: "Weinberger and I were the only ones against it. . . . it was clear to me by the time we went out that the president, the vice president [and others present] all had one opinion and I had a different one and Cap shared it."

Of the same meeting Weinberger testified: "I made [the usual] arguments with increasing force but apparently less persuasion, and George Shultz did the same thing."[3] When Weinberger was indicted in 1992 for misleading Congress, among papers released with the indictment was a note about the January 7 NSC meeting, in which the secretary of defense said that President Reagan had decided to "go with" the proposal to exchange four thousand

---

*Regan and James Baker III had exchanged positions after the 1984 election, Baker becoming secretary of the Treasury.

TOWs for hostages and that Casey, Meese, Poindexter, "and VP" also favored the scheme.[4]

Of this crucial meeting Bush later said that he did not remember "any strenuous objections." If he had heard Shultz and Weinberger "express opposition strongly, I would have had a stronger view."[5]

Ten days later, on January 17, 1986, the vice president also was recorded as present when Reagan signed another "finding," this one accompanied by a memorandum noting that Shultz and Weinberger "do not recommend [the president] proceed with this plan" (arms sales to Iran). On this memo, initialed by Poindexter, he noted in handwriting: "President was briefed verbally from this paper. Vice President, Don Regan and Dan Fortier were present."[6]

On February 1, 1986, Poindexter sent a memo to McFarlane about the status of the Iran "initiative" and noted, "President and vice president are solid in taking the position that we have to try." And though "the Secretaries oppose," Casey, Meese, Regan, and himself were "fully on board this risky option."[7]

Two years later, on January 26, 1988, Shultz said on the CBS program *This Morning* that Bush had been at the January 7, 1986, meeting when he (Shultz) had "strongly opposed the initiative." Attorney General Ed Meese and Poindexter also testified that Bush attended the NSC meeting on January 7, 1986.

More directly, in Israel on July 29, 1986, Bush and his aide, Craig Fuller, were briefed by Amiram Nir, a counterterrorism expert for the Israeli government. Fuller's notes (initialed "CF" about a week later, on August 6) disclose that Nir did not hesitate to talk about arms for hostages—raising the question, for instance, whether weapons should be delivered all at once for the release of all hostages, or whether some should be exchanged for only some hostages, in a sort of progressive arrangement. Fuller noted that the vice president made no commitments and gave no directions but thanked Nir for pursuing the initiative despite all "doubts and reservations."

Bush has testified that he did not fully understand Nir's representation. Maybe not, but Fuller's notes make clear that *he* understood it well enough.[8]

Nor, in 1988, could Bush remember much about that NSC meeting on January 7, 1986, at which Shultz had spoken—"as forcefully as I could," he said—against arms for hostages. In 1988 Bush was openly a presidential candidate, indeed the front-runner to succeed Reagan, so his views were of more than ordinary interest. But on January 25, 1988, he said in a rancorous interview with Dan Rather of CBS: "I've heard George Shultz be very, very forceful. If I [had been] there . . . I would have remembered that."

In another revealing remark to Rather, Bush came close to admitting that he knew the initiative was about arms for hostages. "I went along with it—because you know why, Dan . . . when I saw Mr. Buckley [one of the hostages in Lebanon] being tortured to death, later admitted as a CIA chief. So if I erred, I erred on the side of trying to get those hostages out of there."

Bush later wrote with apparent candor that there were "some signals along the way that the Iran initiative was headed for trouble." Whatever they were, he seems not to have included in that category the "serious doubts" of Shultz and Weinberger. If he'd known about those "and asked the President to call a meeting of the NSC, [Reagan] might have seen the project in a different light, as a gamble doomed to fail."[9]

This statement ignores the fact that there *was* an NSC meeting, on January 7, 1986, that thrashed out the pros and cons of the initiative, with the secretaries of state and defense strongly in opposition and Vice President George Bush at the table. The statement also raises the question of how Bush could *not* have known about the secretaries' "serious doubts." It also puts Bush in much the same position that Ronald Reagan claimed for himself in his television address—favoring a strategic initiative to improve relations with Iran but, rather incredibly, not realizing that the initiative was "deteriorating" into an arms-for-hostages deal.

That's the implication, too, of Bush's reaction after he was finally briefed on the "big picture" on December 20, 1986, by David Durenberger, Republican of Minnesota, then the chairman of the Senate Intelligence Committee. After that briefing, Bush wrote in *Looking Forward,* he had "the feeling . . . that I'd been deliberately excluded from key meetings involving details of the operation."[10]

It's possible, however, that he actually knew more about Iran-contra than did the supposed master of the administration, Ronald Reagan. At least one account credits Bush with trying to talk Reagan out of holding what turned out to be a messy and suspiciously inaccurate news conference on November 19, 1986. The day before the president's disastrous meeting with reporters, as this story has it, Bush went to the Oval Office and in front of Reagan, Attorney General Meese, and Donald Regan, urged the president to put off the news conference "till everybody knew what they were supposed to know, what it was they could admit they knew." But Reagan supposedly couldn't understand that he didn't have all the facts or that some he did have were wrong. "Meese thought the Gipper could just deny it—make it all go away in front of the cameras."

The reporters would "*kill* him out there," Bush is said presciently and sadly to have told an old friend, Governor Tom Kean of New Jersey, that night. "Believe me I went in there . . . as hard as I could."[11] But he got exactly nowhere.*

Cohen and Mitchell, in their summary of the report on the Senate-House hearings, point out that there was "no compelling evidence" that Bush had known of the covert resupply of the contras or had played a significant role in the whole affair. Besides, they argue, a vice president lacks "flexibility to express his views" on a controversial administration issue, and not just because of the loyalty and confidentiality he owes to the president. Even in cabinet sessions or administration meetings, when deep divisions exist, "for the vice president to advocate any position might [undercut] the value of his advice should the President reject it, or [compromise] the President's flexibility in reaching a decision by forcing him to avoid embarrassing his own vice president."[12]

That may be generally true, but George Bush also had those one-on-one, no-holds-barred Thursday luncheons, and an uncommonly open door into the Oval Office. Thus he had ample opportunity to inform Reagan, in total privacy, of his misgivings, if any, about the Iran initiative—or at least to remind the president (who had become "consumed"[13] by the desire to free the hostages) of the doubts of others, including the secretaries of state and defense. Bush has given no intimation, even in his later writings, that he took such advantage of his easy personal access to the president.

On the other hand it's possible that he *did* do so, but that the loyalty he extended to the president, not only politically but as part of his lifelong attitude, has precluded his letting it be known. Besides, *he* was the one who was going to have to run for president

*Foreshadowing his 1988 confrontation with Reagan over Noriega. Bush got nowhere either time.

in 1988, and his need for Reagan's support and that of Republican conservatives would have been a powerful factor in his public silence about any private approaches he may have made.

Therefore there may never be a comprehensive answer to the question pointedly raised by Al Haig during his brief presidential candidacy in 1988: "Where was George Bush during the storm? Was he the co-pilot in the cockpit, or was he back in economy class?"

That question was often echoed in less dramatic language by a more prominent candidate, Senator Bob Dole of Kansas. Ironically enough, despite all the agonizing and dissembling, as the 1988 presidential campaign unfolded, "Where was George Bush during the storm?" never became a real issue*—certainly not a serious threat to the climactic, final entry about to be made in his vaunted résumé.

There *were* serious threats in 1988, however. One was Pat Robertson—not that the politically minded evangelist had a real chance to win the Republican nomination, let alone the presidency. But Robertson had a fanatically loyal personal following of conservative Christians, and the money and ability to turn that following on and then turn it out. So when Robertson undertook what was, in fact, an unlikely presidential candidacy, hordes of his fans enthusiastically lined up behind their favorite, making him an easy victor in the so-called Cavalcade of Stars

---

*Owing to the later Weinberger indictment, Bush's actions as vice president during the Iran-contra affair did become a heated question in his 1992 reelection campaign against Bill Clinton.

straw poll in Iowa in the fall of 1987. Vice President Bush, who had invested substantial time and money in the same straw poll, was humiliated and wounded politically. If someone supposed to be the next president couldn't even beat a radio preacher in a small-state contest that didn't really count . . .

Another and more serious problem was the truly serious candidate, Bob Dole of Kansas—a neighbor state to Iowa, with similar agricultural concerns. Telling Iowans that he was "one of [them]," Dole not only came in second in the Cavalcade of Stars, pushing Bush down to third place; the senator then went on to *win* the actual Iowa caucuses in February 1988—with the vice president, who failed to carry even a single county, again finishing in a lowly third place, behind both Dole and Robertson. Iowa, where Bush had done so well in 1980, had proved a grievous, possibly even terminal embarrassment for the vice president and supposed front-runner.

"If there [were] no Robertson," Richard Wirthlin, Dole's poll taker, said, "there would've been only one headline—Dole Beats Bush. As it is, there's two headlines—both of them bad for Bush."[14]

The 1980 result, moreover, was duplicated in reverse—then, eight years earlier, the relatively unknown Bush had upset Ronald Reagan, the front-runner, and gained his fleeting Big Mo; now the less-touted senator from Kansas had sidetracked the supposedly inevitable nomination of Vice President George Bush. Dole immediately surged in the headlines, public opinion, fund receipts, and the polls in New Hampshire—where the next, more important test would come a week later, in the Republican primary, and where, on Friday before the vote on Tuesday, CBS reported a startling Dole lead—32 percent to only 29 for Bush.

In some ways even more threatening—at least for Bush personally—was the "wimp image" that *Newsweek* fastened on him in what should have been a happy event, a cover story in a national magazine. But the headline on the cover, prominent on every newsstand on October 11, 1987, read: "George Bush: Fighting the Wimp Image." Whether there would have been such an image without that cover story may be questioned, but the origins of the image and the story were clear: George Bush's old-family background, the Andover-Yale connection, the Maine estate, the record of appointive jobs rather than election victories, the "white shoe" appearance and manner, the tennis flannels, the rather hokey (even if genuine) efforts to look folksy (eating pork skins, pitching horseshoes), the desperate "lapdog" pursuit of conservative gurus like William Loeb (even after Loeb's death).

To these evidences of wimphood, Bush added a number of verbal stumbles—most notably when, after returning from a visit to China in 1986, he told a *Wall Street Journal* reporter that if a Chinese official who had greeted him warmly had said such things in the seventies, when Bush was the U.S. envoy, "he'd have been in deep doo-doo"—apparently having shrunk at the last moment from the common "deep shit" that many Americans would have used.[15] That delicacy—if that's what it was—was never to be forgotten and seldom forgiven. And even the story of Bush's wimplike silence when challenged in 1980 by the four excluded candidates at the Nashua, New Hampshire, debate was resurrected after nearly a decade, to become part of the wimp image.

Bush raged that his success in the roughhouse Texas oil business, his athletic skills, his heroic war service, should have improved such an image, indeed have prevented it from ever surfacing. His belligerent performance in the interview with

Dan Rather on January 25, 1988, was in part an effort to look tougher and less wimpish.*

Bob Dole also was a war hero, however, with a shattered right arm, a working-class Midwest background, and no hint of wimp about him. And no matter what Bush did or said, *his* wimp image seemed to stick—the notion that he was not tough enough, not decisive enough, too "preppy," too much of a nice guy, a soft rich kid who'd gotten ahead on family and old school ties, fit mostly to be a striped-pants cookie pusher. Bush's wimp image was a classic example of how a plausible perception (for instance, Lyndon Johnson as a "cowboy"), once expressed, can be so often repeated—in the press and in general conversation—that it might as well be a reality. This one could have sent Bush back to Walker's Point; instead anger and resentment may well have stiffened his supposedly weak spine.

Another serious problem, ironically, was Bush's number two spot in the Reagan administration—without which, of course, he might not even have been running. But echoes of the Iran-contra scandal and his own ambiguous role in it crept into the campaign. The gaudy vice presidential apparatus—the limos, the motorcades and motorcycles, the Secret Service, and the swarming staff—seemed a barrier between Bush and the voters, especially in Iowa. George Bush's ingrained idea of loyalty also prevented him from ever differing publicly or importantly with the president—making him appear to have no strong opinions of his own.

---

*Bush asked Rather, referring to a well-known incident of the time, "How would you like it if I judged your career by those seven minutes when you walked off the set in New York?" Afterward, not knowing his microphone was still live, Bush said into it, "[T]hat bastard didn't lay a glove on me" and referred to CBS as "[y]our goddamn network."

Like every vice president who seeks the presidency, Bush had to bear the onus for everything about the administration that had offended voters, while being unable to take credit for its triumphs. His deference to the Gipper and all his dogged efforts to show that he, too, was a conservative deserving of conservative support—in fact, the president's right-hand man—had failed to win him the true allegiance of the Republican Right. Too many of its members accepted the wimp image—and remembered, not fondly, the "moderate" challenger of 1980 with his "voodoo economics" wisecrack.

The Reagan administration, in its late stages, also provided some politically damaging headlines. Attorney General Meese, for instance, faced certain ethical problems and the investigation of a special prosecutor, on which the news promptly focused. Meese refused to resign until the prosecutor's report stopped just short of recommending his indictment—again providing newspapers and TV with a story they couldn't resist.

Donald Regan, the former White House chief of staff, who had been forced out of office, published a vindictive book in which he charged Nancy Reagan with being a devotee of astrology, with the implication that the alignment of the stars had been allowed to affect her husband's schedule and activities. The press reacted like a kid in a candy shop, and the astrology story became another challenge to Bush's loyalty and his campaign.

The Great Communicator himself suffered the lowest poll figures of his tenure and publicly tried to negotiate Manuel Noriega out of Panama. Noriega declined to go, but one result of Reagan's effort was the disclosure that the CIA once had had the drug king–dictator on its payroll as an informer—including the period in the seventies when George Bush had been DCI. Bush shook off allegations of personal complicity with Noriega only by staging a minibreak with Reagan, declaring that he, Bush, would never negotiate with a drug dealer.

It was mainly the Iowa caucuses and Bob Dole, however, that made George Bush, on the eve of the 1988 New Hampshire primary, no longer seem to be the inevitable Republican presidential nominee. And anyway, it was a historical fact that no sitting vice president had been elected directly to the presidency since Martin Van Buren succeeded Andrew Jackson in 1836, a century and a half earlier.

As it had with Ronald Reagan in 1980, defeat in Iowa—with the New Hampshire primary just around the corner—caused Bush to reevaluate his campaign and his strategy. The limos and the motorcades virtually disappeared in New Hampshire. Taking local advice from Governor John Sununu and others, Bush seized every opportunity to meet and greet people in small groups, roaming widely through shopping malls and factories, wearing wool shirts and earflaps. He tried to respond in the pork-skin mode to the omnipresent wimp image, having himself photographed driving an eighteen-wheeler and a forklift. More significantly he finally "went negative"[16] on television.

To do so was not a quick or an easy decision for the son of Prescott Bush. But in New Hampshire, with only a few days to go before the voting, everything was on the line—"after seven years of careful building, after twenty million dollars spent, after all the briefings, coaching, debate books, the cautious positioning, luxuriant staffing, the hundreds of speeches, the thousands of events . . ."[17] A loss in New Hampshire would be disastrous. Even so Bush hesitated.

The specific question was about an attack ad that Roger Ailes, the campaign television adviser, had prepared on his own, without direct authorization from George Bush. It pictured Bob Dole with two faces, looking at each other. After the prominently displayed word "Straddled," numerous issues were listed. The word changed to the present-tense "Straddle" as "Taxes" flashed on the screen, then became "He Can't Say No."

A narrator proclaimed: "Bob Dole straddles, and he just won't promise not to raise taxes. And you know what that means."

Bush, viewing a tape of the ad, expressed doubt but did not make a firm decision; he wanted to be sure the charges were provable. He was assured they were, owing to Dole's Senate record and his speeches. The pressures to run the ad were strong—Mrs. Bush, George junior on the telephone, campaign strategist Lee Atwater, Ailes himself—all wanted the ad to go on the air, and some advisers openly said it was needed to rescue the campaign (at least in New Hampshire, perhaps nationally).

On Friday before the Tuesday primary, former secretary of state Al Haig withdrew from his floundering presidential campaign and endorsed Bob Dole, then shook hands with Dole in a scene that dominated TV. The CBS preprimary poll figures—Dole, 32 percent; Bush, 29—also became public that day. Even Bush's own poll numbers turned sour: Bob Teeter, the poll taker, who opposed the Ailes ad, said the vice president was trailing by five points but insisted the situation was not irreversible—there were just too many undecideds. But there was no more time to debate, not if the Bush campaign was to "make air" with the two-faced Dole ad in time to influence the voting. If it didn't, New

Hampshire might be gone—and maybe the whole campaign and the presidency with it.

No wonder, therefore, that Bush finally gave in—though no one seems to remember his actual words. Atwater, Ailes, and Sununu went to work. Even on a weekend they got the ad on New Hampshire's only television channel, and on one in Boston that reached all over the state. At a cost of hundreds of thousands of dollars, they got the two-faced Dole ad aired in New Hampshire eighteen times in less than three days—the crucial three days before the voting.

Bob Dole unwittingly helped in his own political execution. At a final candidate debate, televised from St. Anselm College, one of the also-ran candidates, Pete duPont of Delaware, thrust into Dole's hands a copy of a standard no-tax statement, demanding that he sign it. Dole was a political veteran too cagey to rule out a tax increase a year or more in the future ("never say never"); he stared at the paper a moment, then, in full view of the New Hampshire television audience, handed it back to duPont unsigned—wisely perhaps but politically, in New Hampshire, a shot in the foot.

The next day, when the polls closed, Dole learned that, by nine decisive points, he had lost a primary he probably should have won. The Bush campaign had been saved at the last minute. For Bob Dole, who had disliked and disdained George Bush since 1970 and who, for a few fleeting days, had thought *he* would be Reagan's successor, that was bad enough: the euphoria of victory in Iowa, of momentarily overtaking Bush's lead in New Hampshire, all blasted away in a single weekend, and—as Dole thought—by one misleading TV ad. But that was not the end of the affair.

The last event of primary day was a joint appearance by Bush and Dole on NBC with Tom Brokaw, Bush the winner in the New York studio and Dole the loser in his hotel room in New Hampshire.

"Senator," Brokaw said into Dole's earpiece, "any message for the vice president?"

Dole was staring directly into the camera as he answered bluntly:

"Yeah. Stop lying about my record."

That was all. But it was enough for Brokaw's national audience to draw the plausible conclusion that Bob Dole was, indeed, the "hatchet man" his critics claimed. He was never to shed the epithet, in its way as damaging—and as misleading—as Bush's wimp image.

After that Bush had relatively smooth sailing, winning every state on Super Tuesday, Dole hanging in as a candidate only pro forma. On the Democratic side, however, the primary battle continued, narrowing down to Governor Michael Dukakis of Massachusetts and Jesse Jackson, the first black presidential candidate to survive into the final primaries. Dukakis proved to be the last man standing, however, and was anointed as the Democratic presidential nominee at the party's national convention in Atlanta. Democratic delegates, eager to see the last of Ronald Reagan, laughed at Ann Richards's "silver-foot-in-mouth" quip and went home somewhat overconfident, as Dukakis's lead in the polls ranged sometimes as high as sixteen points.

Those numbers made the Bush campaign nervous, but no one would have known it from President Reagan's demeanor. First he failed to appear at a Bush rally where he'd been expected to endorse his vice president in fulsome words provided by Bush's own speechwriters. Then, at a dinner honoring Reagan himself—not Bush—the president concluded a happy review of his two terms with an "endorsement" so limp that a less gentlemanly man than George Bush might have wondered whether his nearly eight years of unrelenting loyalty to his chief had been worthwhile.

Reagan, of course, read off the famous résumé, but then added only: "I'm going to work as hard as I can to make Vice President Bush the next President of the United States."

This was Bush's reward? Washington rumor had it that Nancy Reagan, as always protective of "Ronnie," had ordered out of the president's speech anything that might have detracted from what she considered *his* moment. George Bush surely would have considered that bad form, a lack of due loyalty—had he been a man able to believe that people he considered his friends would act that way.

Not until opening night of the Republican National Convention in New Orleans, with Bush already far behind in the polls, did the President lay on something like a boffo endorsement. George Bush, he told the delegates in words not too well-chosen, was "someone who's not afraid to speak his mind . . . never runs away from a fight, never backs away from his beliefs, and never makes excuses."

Even then Reagan apparently could not resist a final moment of personal glory. To explosive Republican cheers, he trotted out a surefire line: "George . . . one personal request. Go out there and win one for the Gipper!"

CHAPTER FIVE

ON THE EVENING of October 13, 1988, a mostly Democratic crowd gathered in the Century Club on Forty-third Street in New York to celebrate the birthday of one of the best-known among them: John Kenneth Galbraith, the witty Harvard economics professor and author, who had left academia in the early sixties to serve as President Kennedy's ambassador to India.

By chance—the birthday party had been set weeks earlier—October 13 turned out to be the night of the second televised debate between the presidential candidates, Vice President George Bush for the Republicans and Governor Michael Dukakis of Massachusetts for the Democrats. By October, Dukakis—who, that summer, had mistakenly focused mostly on his state responsibilities—had lost much of his early lead in the polls, under blistering negative attack from Bush. The governor, moreover, had failed to respond forcefully, and had developed a reputation for lack of warmth and emotion.

Those who wanted to attend the party for Galbraith also wanted to see the debate, many hoping for a strong Dukakis recovery. A number of TV sets were placed about the Century's clubrooms, and dinner was scheduled to follow rather than precede the debate. It was being broadcast from Los Angeles but in East Coast prime time.

The first debate question that night, addressed to Dukakis and asked by Bernard Shaw of CNN, concerned one of the most volatile and emotional issues in American society. The question and its answer may well have decided the presidential election nearly a month before the voting—scheduled for November 8:

SHAW: Governor, if Kitty Dukakis were raped and murdered, would you favor an irrevocable death penalty for the killer?

DUKAKIS: No, I don't, Bernie. And I think you know that I've opposed the death penalty during all of my life. I don't see any evidence that it's a deterrent, and I think there are better and more effective ways to deal with violent crime. We've done so in my own state . . . one of the reasons why we have had the biggest drop in crime of any industrial state . . . the lowest murder rate of any industrial state . . .

A sort of collective groan rose from the Democrats gathered in the Century Club, as their nominee droned on in the same dry and unemotional tone to discuss the so-called war on drugs. As political buffs most of them realized instantly that Dukakis had missed a great opportunity—committing instead an irretrievable blunder—perhaps had even lost the election. How could he have been so calm, so lawyerly, so pedantic about rape and murder?* Of his own wife? How could he have missed what was really an opportunity to show that he was not cold and unemotional—that he *cared,* not only about Kitty Dukakis, but about crimes most Americans considered savage? Didn't he?

---

*Actually Dukakis had stated sound, if disputed, arguments against capital punishment. It was not the substance of his answer that wounded him, but his lack of emotion and his professorial demeanor.

Bush, in rebuttal, of course reiterated that he was *for* the death penalty (both candidates' basic views had been established earlier in the campaign), because "some crimes are so heinous, so brutal, so outrageous." Weeks later the irrepressible Willie Brown, another opponent of capital punishment, then Democratic majority leader of the California assembly, later mayor of San Francisco, told me what *he* would have said in answer to Shaw's question: "I'd find the killer and strangle him with my own hands. And then would you be for the death penalty for *me?*"

Dukakis said nothing of the kind, to the disgust of millions of voters, including many who wanted to be his supporters. And as many Democrats in the Century Club that night gloomily predicted, the governor went on—mostly in the same low key, as if teaching a civics class, never really answering Bush's charges—to lose the election by the substantial margin of eight percentage points. When the Democratic Convention had nominated him in July 1988, his lead in the polls had been in double digits.

On November 8 George Bush carried forty states and 426 electoral votes—and had what must have been the private satisfaction of settling an old score from the 1970 Texas senatorial race. The victor in that year's election, Lloyd Bentsen, had been the Democrats' vice presidential nominee, and he, too, went down with the Dukakis ship (though owing to a peculiar Texas elections custom, Bentsen did win another term in the Senate).

Bentsen had had one of the Democrats' few triumphal moments in his television debate with Bush's surprise vice presidential nominee Senator Dan Quayle, a Republican from the "heartland" state of Indiana. Bush had chosen the youthful and handsome but largely undistinguished Quayle against the advice of many on his team—though not that of the influential Ailes, basic author of the crucial New Hampshire primary victory. The vice president thought Quayle would be telegenic and would appeal to Republican conservatives, to the other heartland states, to younger voters, and to women, among whom Bush suffered a "gender gap" in the polls. (A joke of the time had it that he reminded every divorced woman of her first husband.)

Quayle proved, however, to be vulnerable on several scores—he had not served in Vietnam, joining a national guard unit instead; he was prone to verbal buffoonery ("I love California; I practically grew up in Phoenix."); he lacked national campaign as well as governing experience; and he was obviously rattled by his new eminence and responsibility—on television, said one critic, he looked like "a deer caught in the headlights." Bush loyally stood by him—"loyalty down," in this case, as it had been "loyalty up" to Reagan—but polls showed that Quayle was "a drag" on the ticket.

Dukakis also had had trouble choosing a running mate. He came under heavy pressure to name the runner-up in the primaries, Jesse Jackson, much as Reagan, on the Republican side, had turned to George Bush in 1980. But Jackson was black and liberal; so, despite Jackson's primary victories, Dukakis made the more conventional choice of Bentsen, who was expected to balance the Massachusetts governor's liberalism and to help carry Texas and other southern states.*

Quayle occasionally responded to criticism by arguing that John F. Kennedy had been no older or more experienced than he.

---

*To hold the black vote despite this choice, Dukakis gave the eloquent Jackson a large role at the Atlanta convention. This, however, offended many conservatives and independents who were watching on TV.

But in his debate with Bentsen, televised from Omaha, Quayle tried that tactic once too often, declaring: "I have as much experience in the Congress as Jack Kennedy did when he sought the presidency."

Bentsen glared and pounced: "Senator, I served with Jack Kennedy. I knew Jack Kennedy. Jack Kennedy was a friend of mine. Senator, you're no Jack Kennedy."

The audience erupted in laughter and cheers. It was the kind of quick and emotional answer* that Dukakis should have given to Bernie Shaw's question on rape and murder. As it was, Quayle never recovered: not in that campaign or in his four years as vice president, not in the losing Bush-Quayle campaign of 1992, and not by 1996 when, four years out of the number two office, he wisely withdrew from—never really having entered—that year's presidential competition. Little has been heard of or from him since.

Bentsen, after four more years in the Senate, became Bill Clinton's first Secretary of the Treasury.

Politically, as Bob Dole found out to his sorrow in New Hampshire, George Bush's wimp image had been misleading. Equally deceptive, whether intentionally or not, had been that early pledge to Bush's Houston minister—after the Goldwaterish Bush Senate campaign in 1964—not again to take positions just "to get elected."

From his entry into political campaigning in 1964, George

*Though Bentsen had been well prepared by his handlers for the opportunity Quayle's remark provided.

Bush had always understood, and sometimes had said,* that a candidate had to do whatever it took to win. Winning was what campaigning was all about. Of course Bush would not do or say anything that would be frowned on at Walker's Point as in bad taste: personal boasting, disloyalty to friends, what Bush called "all that me-me-me" stuff. He meant pointing out an opponent's low character, or something vulnerable in an opponent's background (or, as they say in politics, "building up his negatives" in order to "take him down").

Thus a paradox was about to unfold: a genuinely "nice" man, liked by a host of friends and acquaintances, a model of high-mindedness, was to wage in 1988 one of the most slashing attack campaigns in presidential history.

In June 1988, at the Texas Republican Convention, by then sure of his presidential nomination, Bush gave a huge audience at the Houston convention center a tantalizing taste of what he and his advisers thought it would take to defeat Michel Dukakis. He hit the governor on taxes and defense in sometimes mysterious phrases ("his foreign policy views born in Harvard Yard's boutique would cut the muscle of our defense") and then got down to his real business:

"Michael Dukakis on crime is standard old-style Sixties liberalism . . . he has steadfastly opposed the death penalty . . . he supported the only state program in the whole country—the

---

*On NBC's *Today* during the last week of the 1992 campaign, Bill Clinton made the explicit charge: "[D]on't forget that Mister Bush has said himself he would do anything to get reelected."

only one—that gives unsupervised weekend furloughs to first-degree murderers."[1] That was only a taste of what was to come in the fall campaign.

In July, at the New Orleans national convention, after Ronald Reagan finally said something enthusiastic about him, Bush, in an acceptance speech written by the talented Peggy Noonan of the White House staff, again speared Dukakis on the tax issue, and added a famous and fateful line: "My opponent won't rule out raising taxes. But I will. And the Congress will push me to raise taxes and I'll say, 'no.' And they'll push, and I'll say, 'no.' And they'll push again, and I'll say to them: Read my lips: no new taxes!' "

It was the best applause line of Bush's campaign, drawing thunderous cheers and whoops from the faithful in the huge New Orleans dome. It was a pledge, too, without which a *faux* conservative—as many Republicans thought of Bush—might not have been able to unify the party of Reagan sufficiently for it to win without Reagan. The planned negative attack on Dukakis—glimpsed in Houston—was ready; but would it have been sufficient to overcome the effects of a divided Republican party?

No one that night, including Bush himself, knew that those words—"Read my lips"—repeated over and over by the press and on television, would be graven on the memories of Republicans, conservative and otherwise, ultimately to become an albatross circling above George Bush's presidency. For the moment the pledge aptly served to unify and energize his party and his campaign. And he was already charging from behind.

Staff work had prepared the ground; the defeat of Dole in New Hampshire had shown the way. As candidate and governor of Massachusetts, Dukakis had left a trail of action and positions that offered a fertile field to political researchers with an eye for vulnerabilities. In the primaries he had emerged relatively late as the likely nominee; the other Democratic candidates did not at first realize they needed to "take down" a relatively unknown East Coast governor. But after the nomination was clearly his, the Bush staff put Dukakis under the microscope and found plenty of wriggling bacilli that could be turned into venomous worms.

There was the pollution of Boston harbor, a scandal right under the nose of a supposed environmentalist. "The Duke's" positions on taxes and spending and on national defense, when fully exposed, would make him look like the kind of soft-headed, tax-and-spend liberal that Ronald Reagan had excoriated. Dukakis had been strongly opposed to the death penalty; and he had fought against mandatory sentences for drug offenders: What would they think of *that* out in the provinces? Dukakis had even vetoed a Massachusetts legislative requirement that schoolchildren recite the Pledge of Allegiance to the flag; and of course, as a liberal Democrat, he was opposed to prayer in the schools.

Potentially most lethal of all was a matter Al Gore—another Democratic presidential contender—had raised with Dukakis in the New York state primary: the Massachusetts policy under which inmates, even convicted murderers, were sometimes given weekend furloughs. Two of them had committed murders during their temporary freedom, Gore said in the debate; but his charge had caused little comment, and Dukakis had gone on to win the New York primary. In Dukakis's home state the *Lawrence Eagle-Tribune* had long hammered on the matter, however; and the governor had consistently supported the furlough policy—though finally acquiescing when the legislature changed the law. Here was striking evidence to suggest that the Democratic nominee had been "soft on crime," and would be soft when in the White House.

With all this material in hand, the Bush staff presented it to a room full of New Jersey Democrats who had voted for Reagan but now supported Dukakis—before, that is, they were told about Willie Horton, a furloughed murderer, a black man who had raped a white woman during his weekend freedom from prison. The "focus group" was told, too, that Dukakis opposed the death penalty, had "vetoed" the Pledge of Allegiance, and was against prayer in the schools. Predictably, "Within ninety minutes, half the group had switched to Bush."[2]

At that point Bush himself—the wimp image still clinging to his shoes—had "negatives" of about 40 percent, twice as high as Dukakis's. What to do, therefore, was an open-and-shut case, not only to advisers like Ailes and Atwater but also to a candidate prepared to do whatever was necessary to win, who had worked as hard and waited as long as George Bush had, who had seen how Bob Dole had been "taken down" in New Hampshire. He would have to raise Dukakis's negatives, exposing him as a big-spending liberal, soft on crime, weak on patriotism, unconcerned about family values.

Fortunately the record, as it was seen in the Bush campaign, "proved" all that; and against such a target, therefore, Bush could attack in a righteous spirit, in keeping with his personal beliefs. To a man with George Bush's social and family background, his duty was clear. He had to point out to the American people that

Michael Dukakis was unfit to lead them, or to sit in Ronald Reagan's chair in the Oval Office.

Bush went at the job eagerly, wrapping himself in the flag and in robes of experience and conventional values; before long the polls inevitably began to reflect a shift in his favor. The famous Willie Horton TV ad, one of the most damaging and decisive ever shown, was only part of the attack. Opposing school prayer, vetoing the Pledge (a dastardly act emphasized at a factory that made American flags), allowing the pollution of Boston harbor (supposedly the governor's fault alone), joining the American Civil Liberties Union (ACLU; that the governor was a "card-carrying" member evoked old memories of "card-carrying" Communists and damaged the ACLU as well as Dukakis)—all in all the vivid picture of Dukakis painted by George Bush did indeed raise the governor's negatives and quickly take him down.

At first Dukakis did not help his own cause by virtually refraining from presidential campaigning for most of the summer of 1988, focusing instead on being governor of Massachusetts. When he did get into the national fray, Dukakis proved as righteous as Bush, but in the other direction: He refused to respond to charges that he considered negative, that *he* knew, even if voters didn't, were unfair and had no relevance to the presidency. He refused to believe that Bush and the Republicans could win with such tactics—the American people would not stand for it. He also refused to listen to staff advice that he take virtually any action he didn't want to take. Dukakis stubbornly believed in himself, that his way was the right way—as the public's, even other Democrats', doubts rose precipitately.

One effect of Bush's attack campaign was to make the word

"liberal" seem an epithet, almost like "unpatriotic." For much of the campaign Dukakis refused to concede that he was a liberal. Late in the race, however, in California, he finally did. I was in California at the time, writing about the campaign there, and Dukakis seemed to me almost to be making a confession rather than proudly stating a faith. I thought he was only dismaying liberals further and confirming conservatives in their disdain.

Unused to the glaring exposure of a presidential campaign, Dukakis appeared at times to be running for governor or in a state primary. Unwilling to respond to Bush's charges, he seemed almost to concede them. When in the late stages he began finally to overcome or at least to try to deal with such problems, it was too late, and his finishing "surge," if there really was one, fell far short. Dukakis never did seem to understand that the election was not about "competence," as he'd proclaimed at the Atlanta convention—or, if it was, that he showed little of it as a campaigner. In fact the election was about what the American people wanted to believe, what they thought they saw in those who aspired to their highest office. And what they thought they saw in Michael Dukakis was what George Bush repeatedly pointed out—weakness, even in the liberalism by which he once had prospered.

What the voters saw in Bush, on the other hand, was not brilliance or even strength, and certainly not vision. At least in 1988 they saw a man who shared their instincts and their most enduring values—one of which was winning. George Bush had learned how to win.

Victory was not without costs—in addition to the usual mental and physical exhaustion a presidential campaign brings to winner as well as loser. Polls showed that people blamed Bush for the negative tone (some even thought racist, owing to Willie Horton's black skin) of the 1988 campaign. If the campaign was unenlightening on important issues, moreover, that was largely because Willie Horton and the Pledge of Allegiance were *not* important national issues. Besides, Bush's triumph did not give him much of a "mandate" to do anything, other than what might come routinely into the Oval Office. He had not, after all, campaigned to *do* much of anything—only on the proposition that he was a tried and experienced leader, a man of conventional virtue, while his opponent was not to be trusted.

Bush's most ringing promise had been *not* to raise taxes, and even that was somewhat suspect among conservatives—the base of the Republican Party. Four years earlier, in a by-no-means-forgotten speech, he had said that revenue increases might have to be considered if all else failed to reduce the federal deficit. This commonsensical statement aroused further suspicion, among those who were suspicious anyway, that if they read Bush's lips, they might find them really saying "maybe."

In fact Bush's accession to the White House never quite placated the Reagan faithful, the confirmed right-wingers, the religious fundamentalists. They had had no difficulty voting for Bush over Dukakis; but now they had to face up to what they had wrought, and they were vaguely uneasy about it. In Bush's largely forgettable inaugural address, for instance, a few lines of "bomfog"* raised conservative eyebrows: "America is never wholly

---

*The acronym reporters devised for frequent references in Nelson Rockefeller's speeches to the "brotherhood of man and the fatherhood of God." Gradually "bomfog" came to stand for any passage of supposedly uplifting—especially religious—rhetoric.

herself unless she is engaged in high moral principle. We as a people have such a purpose today. It is to make kinder the face of the Nation and gentler the face of the world. My friends, we have work to do."

"Kinder" and "gentler" than what? To many the answer seemed to be the world that Reagan had bequeathed, that George Bush was taking over. Some conservatives even expected, unrealistically, that Bush would simply take Reagan's chair personally—not that he would substitute his own appointees for the entire Reagan administration. William Kristol, who was coming into office as Quayle's chief of staff, observed that "a lot of Bushies were saying, 'We're not going to be like Reagan.' . . . 'Bush isn't like Reagan. He stays awake in meetings.'" The resulting hard feelings among Reaganites, Kristol thought, were "unnecessary" and could have been avoided with "a little outreach and stroking."[3]

This uneasiness didn't surface publicly since, in the first weeks of his presidency, the genial Bush, cavorting with his grandchildren, pitching horseshoes, sometimes cooking out behind the White House, was highly enjoying himself and busily creating a honeymoon public atmosphere about the new administration. I well remember a friend, nominally a Democrat, who was invited to Camp David and spent a weekend pitching horseshoes and otherwise sharing Bush's company. He came back enthusiastic about the new president—not for any particular policy but because George Bush was "such a nice guy."

Almost immediately, however, in Washington, Bush encountered two serious political problems, both at least partially of his own making.

One was the growing scandal surrounding the collapse, or the publicized business difficulties, of many of the nation's savings-and-loan banks—the so-called thrifts, once considered bastions of conservatism and security in the financial world. But that was before changes in regulations governing their operations—in some of which Vice President Bush had been peripherally engaged.* Before, too, the resulting advent of too many fast operators in S & L boardrooms. Both developments allowed and even encouraged the "thrifts" to make questionable loans and move into risky business ventures.

When Paul Volcker became chairman of the Federal Reserve in 1979, with the Carter administration still in office, he found inflation running at 13 percent and promptly tightened the money supply. Recession followed; the prime rate jumped to 21.5 percent, and unemployment to nearly 11 percent. But home mortgages, the major business operation of S & Ls, were at fixed rates that couldn't be raised; at the same time S & L depositors began withdrawing their funds to seek higher returns in the money market or in government bonds. These combined developments squeezed S & L profits; when the Reagan administration took office in 1981, two-thirds of the thrifts were losing money. A number were bankrupt.

Trying to help, and egged on by industry lobbyists, Congress raised federal insurance on S & L accounts to $100,000 from $40,000, when those accounts averaged only about $6,000. Then

---

*Owing to Bush's assignment in the Reagan administration to head a task force on "regulatory relief." He has never been charged with any direct, personal responsibility for the so-called S & L crisis.

the legislators removed controls on what interest S & Ls could charge, and allowed them to lend and invest as they saw fit— including lending to their owners. In the past, they had been restricted to making home mortgage loans. S & L funds began to flow into real estate developments, construction projects, and wildcat schemes of all sorts, as well as into the pockets of owners and speculators attracted by the new possibilities Congress had raised. The Reagan administration mostly looked the other way, but also helped prop up near-insolvent S & Ls—by 1988, it was spending about a billion dollars a month for that purpose.

One of the most famous instances of S & L fraud was that of Lincoln Savings and Loan in Arizona, run by one Charles Keating. Lincoln's ultimate failure is estimated to have cost taxpayers more than two billion dollars. It also implicated the so-called Keating Five, Senators McCain, Glenn, Cranston, Riegle, and DeConcini, to all of whose campaigns Keating had contributed. Their later efforts to help him came to little and seem to have been more improper than illegal; anyway, none of the five was censured or indicted, though Keating himself went to jail.

Dukakis had tried to raise the S & L issue in the 1988 campaign but was not heard through the noise of Bush's attacks. An undocumented report suggests that Bentsen, a former investor in Texas S & Ls, pressured the Democratic nominee to drop the subject. More likely, campaign exposure would have threatened too many members of both parties.

Bush had to confront the S & L crisis, much of which could be traced to the Reagan years, in his first month of office. His son Neil, moreover, was involved as a part owner of Silverado S & L, the failure of which is estimated to have cost taxpayers more than a billion dollars. No indictment of Neil Bush resulted, perhaps because he was guilty of nothing illegal.

President Bush and Congress settled on a $157 billion "bailout" plan for the industry; and in August 1989, it was approved in the cumbersomely named Financial Institutions Reform, Recovery and Enforcement Act (FIRREA). The Resolution Trust Corporation also was formed to dispose of failed S & Ls, some at fire-sale prices, and the $157 billion bailout was financed by thirty-year bonds, whose ultimate cost—depending on interest rates between 1990 and 2020—would be far higher than the face amount of the bailout. No matter how high the costs, taxpayers are locked into them until 2020.

The other problem Bush had to face quickly was more direct—his nomination of former senator John Tower, Republican of Texas, to be secretary of defense. A lack of what businessmen call "due diligence" may have been at fault here.

A veteran of four Senate terms, Tower had been for a year Reagan's chief negotiator in the strategic arms limitation talks (SALT), and seemed sufficiently qualified. He was unpopular, however, in the Senate, where he was recalled unfavorably as a near-dictatorial chairman of the Armed Services Committee. Twice divorced, Tower also had a well-known—perhaps exaggerated—reputation in Washington and Texas for drinking, and was accused of overfondness for the opposite sex. All this, as well as the opposition of the current Armed Services Committee chairman, Sam Nunn, Democrat of Georgia, seems to have been underestimated by Bush and by his inexperienced (in Washington) chief of staff, former Governor Sununu of New Hampshire.

No new president needs a confirmation fight with the Senate just as he takes office, and few have had to undergo one. Bush probably could have avoided such a battle had he named the experienced Brent Scowcroft,* who wanted the job, to be secretary of defense[4] instead of national security adviser. But the supreme value the president always placed on loyalty, while in the first instance it aided Tower, ultimately worked against Bush himself. Tower had not only been elected in 1962 as the first Republican senator from Texas (an inspiration to Bush's own efforts in 1964 and 1970); he had strongly backed both Reagan-Bush tickets and had been an early Bush supporter in 1988. Perhaps more important, in 1986 Tower had chaired the so-called Tower Commission named by Reagan to look into the actions of the NSC and its staff during the Iran-contra affair. The Tower Commission report, issued in 1987, had raised questions about the White House chief of staff, Donald Regan, that led to his forced resignation; but it had not pointed an accusing finger at the vice president, for which he was no doubt grateful.

The Tower nomination soon was in difficulty; drinking and sex charges were publicly debated, and further allegations suggested that Tower was too close to certain defense contractors. They had paid him $750,000 in the years since he had left the Senate—for doing what, he never quite explained. Bush stuck solidly with his beleaguered nominee, sacrificing much of the political respect and goodwill most new presidents have been able to exploit. But in the end, as the Armed Services Committee prepared to vote on Tower, Chairman Nunn said, probably deci-

*Scowcroft had been national security adviser under President Gerald Ford.

sively: "I cannot in good conscience vote to put an individual at the top of the chain of command when his history of excessive drinking is such that he would not be selected to command a missile wing, a [Strategic Air Command] bomber squadron or a Trident missile submarine."[5]

The committee then voted on strict party lines, 11 to 9, to reject the nomination. President Bush, in Japan for the funeral of Emperor Hirohito, loyally vowed to carry the fight to the Senate floor. He did, and Tower was defeated there, too, by 53 to 47.* It may only be speculated whether Democratic resentment of Bush's campaign tactics in 1988 influenced Tower's fate in 1989.

Bush had not just lost an original cabinet choice, a rare setback for a new president, who has a presumptive right to choose his own aides; he also had lost political "face" and some degree of respect for his political muscle and judgment. Every president needs to look strong on taking office and when presenting his first legislative proposals; Bush came near flunking that test, because he stayed too long and loyally with John Tower's nomination.

The controversy blurred Bush's prospects and inevitably recalled the ill-advised choice of Dan Quayle; questions were raised, too, about the new chief of staff, Sununu, a small-state governor with no Washington background, who had been confident that Tower would be confirmed. Bush had picked Sununu, Quayle, and Tower over the private objections of close advisers, and ultimately would be accused of being overloyal to all three.

*The Senate then consisted of fifty-five Democrats and forty-five Republicans.

That first trip abroad, to Hirohito's funeral,* suggested that Bush as president would be as preoccupied as he always had been with making and keeping friends. In "only two days in Japan, [he] scheduled 19 meetings with kings, presidents and prime ministers of countries ranging from France to Saudi Arabia to Singapore. But since he was unprepared to get into matters of substance, many of the meetings lasted only fifteen to twenty-five minutes, including opening pleasantries and time for translation."[6]

Despite the Tower setback, and the brutal Chinese repression in June 1989 of a student demonstration in Beijing's Tienanmen Square—about which Bush could do little, and was generally seen to do little—the first year of the Bush administration at home and especially abroad was remarkably successful. It was a year topped off by the fall of the Berlin Wall on November 9 and by the brief, popular war with Panama in December 1989 (about both of which, more later).

These events shored up the president's right flank after Tienanmen Square. Conservatives were largely quiescent anyway, owing to the "read my lips: no new taxes" pledge, and to the efforts of the gregarious South Carolina conservative Lee Atwater, the new Republican Party chairman. Atwater was quick both to fend off recurrent stirrings of discontent on the right and to urge the president to take certain steps—such as backing a proposed constitutional amendment to ban flag-burning—that would please his conservative backers. As 1990 opened, Bush's approval

*The Japanese might have been insulted if the U.S. head of state had sent the controversial Vice President Quayle to the funeral of Japan's head of state.

rating in one poll reached 79 percent, including 74 percent of black voters and 66 percent of Democrats—amazing numbers for a Republican president.

In March 1990, however, the likable Atwater was diagnosed with a brain tumor and died shortly thereafter, long before what should have been his time. In a sense Atwater's loss marked the beginning of a troubled period for the Bush administration. The Chinese continued to be defiant about Tienanmen Square. The federal deficit, which had ballooned under Reagan's "voodoo" formula of reduced taxes and increased defense spending, continued to grow. Bush's proposed new budget got short shrift in Congress, and Democrats refused to relieve him of his no-new-taxes pledge by passing needed increases on their own; they insisted that Bush would have to join them and share voter reaction, if there was to be any tax increase for an attack on the deficit.

In May 1990 Bush summoned congressional leaders to the White House to work out a bipartisan deficit reduction plan. When he argued that Congress had the responsibility for revenues, House Majority Leader Richard Gephardt responded with sarcasm: "It's the first time in this century we've seen a President want to give power to Congress."[7]

Everybody—save possibly the Republican Right—knew that no assault on the deficit would be successful without new taxes. The logic was inexorable; and at breakfast with the leaders on June 26, 1990, Bush finally agreed to break his "read my lips" pledge. That day Press Secretary Marlin Fitzwater placed a White House statement, agreed to by congressional leaders of both parties, on a pressroom bulletin board. It called for a variety of steps to curb the deficit—but the one that counted was second on the list: "tax revenue increases."

Republican conservatives were outraged by the prospect of new taxes after all; some were pledged as solidly as Bush to oppose any such thing. Republicans generally were dismayed by the blow to Bush's credibility. He had broken one of the loudest, most ironclad political pledges ever made—offered to a party convention before a national television audience—a promise without which he might conceivably not have been able to win the presidential election. With that one action—breaking his pledge—the president of the United States brought into question both his personal reliability and his political judgment (in making such a promise in the first place, and breaking it in the second). Here, if ever, was a case of "chickens coming home to roost"—doing what Bush thought he had to do to win the election had sharply contradicted what he had to do to govern the nation.

Eventually the agreed-upon budget deal provided $140 billion in new tax revenues, with the deficit to be reduced by about $500 billion over five years. Ed Rollins, the professional who had been engaged to lead the effort to reelect Republicans to the House of Representatives, noted that more than a hundred of them had voted against the budget package. As a result Rollins took the unprecedented—almost the unthinkable—step of writing a memo to his candidates, advising them that, if they wanted to win, they should separate themselves from Bush, the Republican president, on the tax and deficit issue.

Bush vainly tried to fire Rollins for disloyalty—though, in fact, Rollins had only done what he thought *he* had to do to win House elections, just as Bush had done in the New Hampshire primary and in the presidential campaign. And in the November 1990 midterm elections, marked by one of the lowest Republican turnouts in any congressional campaign, voters dealt what was clearly a rebuff more to the president for his broken tax pledge than to Ed Rollins for his "disloyalty." Republicans lost a Senate seat and eight more in the House; and the result might have been worse had it not been for encouraging news from a tottering Communist empire.

CHAPTER SIX

ALMOST NO ONE, except perhaps some in the narrow worlds of scholars and spies, predicted the fall of the Berlin Wall in November 1989. Even fewer expected the collapse of the Soviet empire in Eastern Europe, followed by the disintegration of the Soviet Union itself, in 1991.

Most Americans, in the years following World War II, had grown accustomed, even reconciled, to the idea of a world divided into West and East: the United States and its allies versus a belligerent Communist bloc ruled by the Union of Soviet Socialist Republics—popularly known to Americans as "Russia," though the actual Russia was only a constituent republic of the USSR. The Cold War between these adversaries came to seem natural, only to be expected, like the seasons. (The so-called Third World of neutral, mostly underdeveloped nations, hardly counted—certainly not militarily. Dwight Eisenhower's secretary of state, John Foster Dulles, had even declared neutralism—reluctance to support the West—"immoral.")

An "evil empire," Ronald Reagan later called the Communist world, and most Americans agreed. "We will bury you," Nikita Khrushchev, one of the Soviet Union's most energetic leaders, had said; few doubted that the Soviets would try. The Soviet Union itself was the other superpower, covering one-sixth of the world's land area and commanding unlimited manpower. It was new and therefore backward in some ways (and "atheistic," the most damning charge in American eyes), but could deploy over-whelming military might and had absolute, ruthless control of its people and of satellites in Eastern Europe and elsewhere.

In the late fifties many in the West believed that the Soviet Union might even be the world's most advanced nation in the science of rocketry—clearly, at least, it was the first to send a satel-lite or a man into space. By the eighties Soviet production was 20 percent of the world's total and that of the Communist na-tions as a whole was about a third of the world's total output of goods and services.

Western military and political leaders focused mostly on their worst nightmare—that a vast Soviet army might someday sweep irresistibly across Western Europe; in a speech leaked to the West in 1956 or 1957, Marshal Georgy Zhukov actually had said that Soviet war plans "called for reaching the English Channel on the second day of hostilities."[1] Ordinary Americans, primed by scary news reports and dozens of doomsday books and films, were far more alarmed by the specter of fleets of Soviet planes carrying atomic bombs or, later, of nuclear-tipped Soviet missiles, swarm-ing over the North Pole to destroy a United States and its people that had been regarded for centuries as too isolated by oceans and continents to be attacked from abroad.*

Fear of atomic or nuclear war was almost universal. On De-cember 8, 1953, addressing the UN General Assembly, President

---

*"From mid-1946 onwards every political and military development fuelled the demand for intelligence" on the capabilities and intentions of the Soviet Union. Richard Helms, *A Look over My Shoulder: A Life in the Central Intelligence Agency* (New York: Random House, 2003), p. 93.

Eisenhower eloquently observed that the world's peoples—not just Americans—were gripped in "the hopeless finality of a belief that two atomic colossi are doomed malevolently to eye each other indefinitely across a trembling world."

American schoolchildren were taught to duck beneath their desks and put their heads between their knees in the event of an atomic attack—futile advice nevertheless taken seriously. American housewives stocked up on canned goods and bottled water in their basements during the Cuban missile crisis of 1962. Admired political figures like Governor Nelson Rockefeller of New York solemnly advised their countrymen to build backyard bomb shelters, and worldwide agitation for an end to nuclear testing with its deadly "fallout" became commonplace. When President Reagan and his CIA director, William Casey, talked about "rolling back the Soviet empire," they heightened fears of a third world war.[2]

Even during the most frightening years of the Cold War, however, contradictory signs had been there to see. President Kennedy, for instance, was forced to admit in 1961, after extravagant Democratic campaign claims in 1960, that there was no "missile gap"; the United States was far ahead of the Soviet Union in that arcane new area of warfare. Neither the Korean War in the 1950s nor the Vietnam War in the 1960s and 1970s exploded into global nuclear warfare; both sides were obviously wary of that possibility. Both entered into arms limitation pacts, as well. The Soviet-American nuclear test ban treaty of 1961, though more an environmental than an arms control agreement, did limit atmospheric testing and therefore the fallout menace. The 1970s and President Nixon even brought a welcome, though deceptive, détente in the Soviet-American arms race.

The uneasy stability of this "balance of terror"—though it had prevailed for forty years—was illusory. In the 1980s—probably even earlier—the Soviet Union was no longer the unshakable powerhouse that it had seemed, and unrest was rising within its empire of satellite states. In both cases economic decline was a major cause. In the years 1971 to 1975, for instance, the Soviet Union's gross national product (GNP) dropped to only 3.7 percent average annual growth, from the 5.3 percent annual average of the period 1966 to 1970. Growth had been 10 percent or more in the early postwar years.*

In 1973 production of goods and services around the world was growing at the rate of 6.2 percent annually—clearly leaving the Soviet Union behind. Its agricultural productivity, in particular, was slipping fast; the figures for Soviet grain production from 1981 to 1986 were so bad that Moscow suppressed them. An aging population—7 percent of the Soviet people had been sixty or older in 1939; by 1987 the over-sixty cohort had doubled to 14 percent—meant a smaller work force and a shrinking ratio of actual workers to the elderly and retired. The economic situation of the Soviet Union was worsened, moreover, by huge defense spending—5 to 6 percent of its annual GNP, the CIA estimated,† but perhaps twice that, according to some defectors.

This seems quixotic today, but the Soviets apparently thought they could match or better the United States in "strategic"—nuclear—forces, so that Washington could never use *its* strate-

---

*All Soviet statistics were subject to manipulation, hence were suspect in the West.

†Team B thought this estimate much too low.

gic forces for anything but responding to a nuclear attack on the United States. This buildup would effectively mean that an overwhelming Soviet march across Europe with conventional forces would deter the Americans from responding with nuclear weapons.

The processes of decline in the Soviet behemoth—including satellite countries seething with discontent in the seventies and eighties—continued, for reasons understood mostly by "experts" in East and West. The Soviet Union itself was wedded to a command economy,* to defense spending, and to the heavy industrial production insisted upon by Stalin. That approach was unsuited, in later years, to the fast-changing technologies of market societies and could not keep up with developments that flourished elsewhere—in computers, for instance, in software and communications electronics, and in automobile design.

Soviet production managers were protected from competition at home and abroad. The bureaucrats who made economic choices were not providing sufficient funds for modernizing manufacturing or satisfying consumers. As economic decline continued, worker morale was low; alcoholism was on the increase; housing was scarce; collective farming was inefficient; and heavy food importation combined with a decline in sales of oil abroad produced a dangerous trade imbalance. The ruble declined in value almost to nothing outside the Soviet Union. Environmental degradation became steadily more threatening; in

---

*Economic decisions were driven not by market demand but by cumbersome government bureaucracies issuing solemn decrees and mostly unrealistic "five-year plans."

Poland, for instance, dependence on coal was a major reason why only 1 percent of the nation's water was suitable for drinking; 25 percent of the land around Kraków was unusable—poisoned by chemical and metal pollution.

Perhaps even more debilitating was the growth of "corruption" within the ruling Communist parties—their leaders regaling themselves with vacation residences, limos, pensions, perquisites of all kinds. In Yugoslavia the Communist dissident Milovan Djilas defined a "new class of owners and exploiters" with special privileges not much different from those of their counterparts in capitalist societies. Communist revolutions to abolish "class," Djilas wrote, actually had *created* a dominant class. And as life for ordinary citizens grew more difficult and economically stagnant, with goods of all kinds scarce and sorry (shoes were produced in quantity in the Soviet Union but of such poor design and quality that even more had to be imported), general resentment of the "new class" grew apace.

All this, more or less inherent in the Soviet system, reached something like a crisis point late in the leadership years of Leonid Brezhnev (1966–1982); and little improvement was seen in the brief succeeding regimes of Yuri Andropov and Konstantin Chernenko, who together led the Soviet Union for only a little more than two successive years. When, on March 15, 1985, the relatively unknown Mikhail Gorbachev was made general secretary of the Central Committee of the Communist Party, the Soviet Union commanded a military establishment thought to be the world's largest; but owing to its technological deficiencies and despite its huge military spending, the Soviets still had no realistic hope of overcoming U.S. strategic forces. More significant, their GNP had a negative growth rate, and Gorbachev's conclusion was unavoidable: "We can't go on like this," he told the Politburo meeting that nominated him.

Only four months earlier, he had predicted that without a flourishing economy, the USSR would not be able to enter the twenty-first century as one of the world's great powers. And so it proved.

Gorbachev was nevertheless a committed party man. He wanted not to abolish "socialism" or the USSR but to prove that they could be as productive as the West, and could reward their citizens materially, just as capitalism did. He wanted not to start anew but to reform the system through his program of *perestroika*. Laws were passed allowing production managers more initiative, and a few joint ventures with foreign companies were authorized. Decrees were issued to improve the quality and timeliness of production. Some cooperatives were permitted. Private land was offered to some farmers—not for sale but to be farmed. There was a crackdown on party favoritism and on alcoholism, and an effort was made to improve incentives—raising the wages of scientific and technical workers by 50 percent, and adjusting other salaries to reflect the quality of work being done.

Crucially, however, Gorbachev did not do away with central economic planning, instead creating superagencies—more bureaucrats—to oversee the ones already in place. To achieve his ambitious goals—a 30 percent increase in productivity by 1990, an 80 to 90 percent increase by 2000—Gorbachev realized that workforce morale would have to rise; this meant that workers, as well as newspapers and television, had to be given more freedom and openness—*glasnost.*

He also understood the necessity for reducing the outsized share of Soviet resources and production devoted to the military; one of his first moves had been a temporary freeze on deployment of intermediate-range missiles. Cuts in military spending required further arms agreements with the United States, and Gorbachev did not shrink from this necessity. He believed, remarkably for a Soviet leader, that the capitalist powers neither wanted war nor were deterred from it only by Soviet military strength. Over military objections, Gorbachev met on arms control with President Reagan in Geneva in 1985, in Iceland in 1986, and in Moscow and the United States in 1987 and 1988. On Governors Island in New York harbor in December 1988, he also renewed acquaintance with Reagan's successor, President-Elect George Bush.

The two had first met when Bush represented the United States at the funeral of Chernenko in 1985. At that time, in "almost a prescription for the way U.S.–Soviet relations would unfold in the years to come," the vice president had cabled his impression of the new party chairman to Reagan: "The gist [of what Gorbachev had said] being as follows—'don't lecture us on human rights, don't attack socialism, but let's each take our case to discussion.'" Even then, at the outset of their relationship, Bush—perhaps sensing a new friend—believed that Gorbachev was offering "man-to-man sincerity."[3]

In their various meetings Reagan and Gorbachev convinced each other that each genuinely wanted to avoid nuclear war and end the arms race—so far had Reagan and the world come from his belief of 1980 that such a war could be won. In the Soviet Union, however, Gorbachev made little progress on *perestroika*— his antialcohol program, for instance, resulting in little but a loss of sales-tax revenues to the government. Consumer goods remained in short supply, further decreasing tax receipts, and—paradoxically—prices were rising (too many rubles chasing too few goods). Planners' demands were still insufficiently attuned to production capabilities; managers were accustomed to being told what to do rather than acting on their own instincts and experience. Growth targets were not even close to being met.

Glasnost, perestroika, military spending cuts, and Gorbachev himself did provoke plenty of opposition—from hardened Communists defending the system on the Right, and from emboldened dissenters attacking it on the Left. His domestic popularity, once high, began to fade even as he was being hailed abroad. In May 1989 he convoked and presided over a televised Congress of People's Deputies, 2,250 members strong, at which dissenters—led by the great physicist and former state prisoner Andrei Sakharov*—were given full voice. They took telling advantage of the opportunity.

Economic reforms, they said, were only cosmetic, and offset by "retrograde measures." The bureaucracy ruled without accountability. Six to eight billion rubles badly needed domestically were being sent annually to Latin America, mostly to Cuba. Sausages and dairy products were dangerously high in chemical content. Twenty percent of the Soviet population lived in ecological disaster areas. The infant mortality rate was higher than in Africa, and life expectancy was lower than in most developed nations.

In February 1989 Gorbachev had withdrawn Soviet troops

*When Sakharov died in December 1989, four days of national mourning were declared for a man named in a poll as the most popular person in the Soviet Union in the twentieth century.

from the stalemated war in Afghanistan—actually a losing war, not least because the United States provided ample numbers of shoulder-fired Stinger missiles to the fiercely resisting Afghan *mujahideen*. Gorbachev then proceeded to nullify the so-called Brezhnev Doctrine—named for the former chairman's declaration in 1968 that any threat to Communist rule anywhere would be "not only a problem of the people of the country in question, but a general problem and concern of all the socialist countries."[4] In keeping with that doctrine, Brezhnev had put together a coalition of socialist nations to suppress with tanks the "Prague Spring" uprising in Czechoslovakia in 1968.

Gorbachev, however, taking note of strong currents of dissent in Poland and Hungary, said in July 1989 that those countries were free to act in "their way" (a jocular press spokesman quickly called this the "Sinatra Doctrine"). It was no joke, however, that Gorbachev's attempted *perestroika*, even if largely unsuccessful at home (though by the end of 1989, each Soviet republic had its own parliament), was spreading to the satellites. So, particularly, was *glasnost*. The Baltic states were even agitating for their independence. But Gorbachev continued to believe that "good Communists" could win the support of the people even in countries restless under socialism. He was quickly disabused of that notion.

In Poland the Communist government again found itself unable to crush the persistent dissident group, Solidarity. In prudence or in panic, government leaders, in roundtable negotiations beginning in February 1989, agreed to allow a legalized Solidarity to put forward a limited but significant number of candidates in coming elections. In midsummer 1989 Solidarity won sweeping victories, became dominant among Polish parties, and was the first opposition party to take part in the government of a satellite state—and that government was the first non-Communist government in Eastern Europe in more than forty years.

That same summer, the American president, George Bush, visited Poland and Hungary for talks with political leaders in both nations. In Poland he met with Lech Wałesa, the leader of Solidarity, and Gen. Wojciech Jaruzelski, the Communist president. Apparently, Bush was instrumental in encouraging Jaruzelski to remain as president and persuading Wałesa to support him, in a somewhat strained but workable coalition government. A year later, in November 1990, Wałesa was elected the first non-Communist president of Poland—and of any Soviet "satellite."

On his return flight to the United States in 1989, Bush—still the inveterate note and letter writer—drafted a personal communication to Gorbachev. He said that the time for a meeting of the two leaders had arrived,* and proposed a no-agenda visit in the United States or elsewhere, not to be called a summit to avoid overexpectations. "I just want to reduce the chances there could be misunderstandings between us," he wrote, characteristically adding: "I want to get our relationship on a more personal basis."[5]

The snowball of change had begun to roll downhill. Hungary, with its long history of dissidence and reform, including the uprising of 1956 and the displacement in 1988 of its veteran Communist leader, János Kádár—and no doubt egged on by events in Poland—moved to become a real, not just a people's, republic. In February the Central Committee announced that it would

*The result was to be the Malta conference in December 1989.

share power in a coalition government of Hungary; in May a dialogue began among all political parties; and in September new parliamentary and presidential elections were announced.

That summer travel restrictions on Hungarians had been relaxed. This had devastating effect in East Germany (the so-called German Democratic Republic [GDR]), Moscow's most solid ally in Eastern Europe. East Germans could travel freely to Poland, Czechoslovakia, and Hungary; in 1989 they poured into Hungary, some being allowed to slip from there across the border into Austria. In September, Hungary formally opened that border, and East Germans crossed it by the thousands, most of them on their way to West Germany. The GDR government panicked, its economy endangered by the huge flight of skilled workers.

East Germany was preparing to celebrate its fortieth anniversary as a state; but the guest of honor, Mikhail Gorbachev, dampened the occasion for Erich Honecker, the GDR's old-line Communist leader. Gorbachev reminded Honecker that the Brezhnev Doctrine was dead—Moscow would no longer send troops to quell disorder in Eastern Europe; there would be no Soviet tanks to crush a "Prague Spring" anywhere. In mid-October the East German politburo deposed Honecker, but further reforms, or promises of reforms, failed to stop huge popular demonstrations, particularly in Leipzig and East Berlin, that were shaking the GDR to its artificial foundations. On November 9 the government, still trying to win the popular loyalty it had never really commanded, announced without fanfare that at midnight, all travel restrictions would be lifted.

East Berliners took that to mean the Berlin Wall would be opened; so did West Berliners; and both gathered that day in huge celebratory crowds on either side of the Wall. Here is how

Time in its November 20, 1989, issue, described what happened "at the stroke of midnight":

> [T]housands . . . let out a roar and started going through [the Wall], as well as up and over. West Berliners pulled East Berliners to the top of the barrier along which in years past many an East German had been killed* while trying to escape; at times the Wall almost disappeared beneath waves of humanity. They tooted trumpets and danced on the top. They brought out hammers and chisels and whacked away at the hated symbol of imprisonment, knocking loose chunks of concrete and waving them triumphantly before television cameras. They spilled out into the streets of West Berlin for a champagne-spraying, horn-honking bash that continued well past dawn, into the following day and then another dawn. As [a local newspaper] would headline: Berlin Is Berlin Again.

Most of the West celebrated, too, if not as wildly as in Berlin; but in Washington, President Bush chose to "play it cool," not wishing either to appear as an instigator of revolt or to raise the likelihood of a violent reaction from Moscow. At a crowded news conference in the Oval Office, with reporters pushing around his desk, Bush was told by Lesley Stahl of CBS that "this is a sort of great victory for our side . . . but you don't seem elated."

"I'm not an emotional kind of guy," Bush replied.

"Well, how elated are you?"

*The number amounted to 192, with about two hundred more "injured by shooting," between August 13, 1961, and November 9, 1989. More than three thousand had been arrested trying to escape. www.dailysoft.com/berlinwall/history/escape.htm.

"I'm very pleased," the president said.[6]

Gorbachev, surprised, was by no means pleased, and reacted as if for the first time he realized the implications of events in Eastern Europe. But for him worse was to come. "The crack in the wall in 1989," as Steven Hayward* wrote, "proved to be the fatal fissure" in the evil empire as a whole.

Already scheduled when the Wall fell was a Bush-Gorbachev meeting in Valletta harbor on the Mediterranean island of Malta—a shipboard conference reminiscent of the Roosevelt-Churchill meeting off Newfoundland in 1942. President Bush particularly liked the idea because he thought meeting the Soviet leader on a ship would make it easier to shut out the press.

Bush could not turn his attention entirely to Eastern Europe and Soviet relations, however, because he was still jousting with China over Tienanmen Square. Western television had captured the scene in Beijing for a worldwide audience, and Congress continued to put pressure on Bush for a strong response; and the United States did become the first nation to impose sanctions (though relatively mild). Months later Bush still was trying to get Chinese leaders to make a gesture to the students that would enable him to restore good relations.

Malta came first, however. Bush consulted widely with Western allies before setting off on November 29—and was sternly advised by Prime Minister Margaret Thatcher of Britain to agree to no defense reductions at all. Upon his arrival, Valletta harbor

*Hayward was a senior fellow at the Pacific Institute of Research, and an adjunct fellow of the Ashbrook Center for Public Affairs at Ashland University in Ashland, Ohio. www.ashbrook.org.

was hit by a storm so severe that the meetings had to be held on the newly refitted Soviet cruise ship *Maxim Gorky,* which was tied up in a secure berth.

Bush pointed out that he had not "jumped up and down on the Berlin Wall" or otherwise gloated over developments in Eastern Europe. Gorbachev said he "appreciated" that and, in a second, smaller meeting, confided to Bush "in the most private way" that Fidel Castro of Cuba had asked him "to help normalize US-Cuban relations." Bush defended the American position on Nicaragua and Cuba and gave a hint that the United States had plans to deal with Manuel Noriega in Panama.*

The storm and resulting rough water in the harbor caused Gorbachev, that night, to cancel his attendance at dinner— swordfish and lobster—on the U.S. cruiser *Belknap.* The next day, again aboard the *Maxim Gorky,* Gorbachev made the flat pledge that "the Soviet Union will under no circumstances start a war" and was ready "no longer to regard the United States as an adversary . . . our relationship is cooperative." He nevertheless feared that internal political pressures might drive the Soviet Union to use force to prevent the Baltic states from seceding. In that case, Bush replied, *his* internal politics were such that the United States "would have to respond to any use of force by the Soviets" in the Baltics.

Scowcroft thought, in the end, that the Malta conference "worked far better" than he had hoped, its major accomplishment having been that each side had clearly presented its attitude "on a whole series of issues." Bush, the expert on friendship,

*The brief U.S. attack on Panama would unfold later that December.

thought that he and Gorbachev "had a lot of common ground" and that the Malta talks had had "a positive effect on [their] personal relationship . . . symbolized in [a] joint press conference— the first ever in US-Soviet relations."[7]

Gorbachev, no doubt with a certain foreboding after the breaching of the Wall, went home to worsening developments in the Soviet Union—and especially in Eastern Europe.

Communist leaders in Prague, facing the same kind of discontent that had caused upheavals in Poland, Hungary, and East Germany, at first tried tough-guy tactics. Demonstrations in 1988 and 1989 culminated in November 1989 in a massive student-led outpouring, with crowds of protesters numbering at least two hundred thousand. The party leader, Miloš Jakeš, and other Communist officials, well able to see which way the wind was blowing, resigned; but the following day's demonstrators numbered an estimated five hundred thousand, demanding a complete end of Communist rule. At about that time half the national population also took part in a two-hour general strike, with the same objective.

All this produced free elections in December 1989; and as the New Year opened, Vaclav Havel, the playwright and a leading dissident, was president of a free Czechoslovakia and, symbolically, the former Communist Alexander Dubcek was chairman of the national parliament. In 1968, Dubcek had led the Prague Spring, the brief, tragic uprising to bring about "communism with a human face."

In the GDR, even under a new and reform-minded leader, Hans Modrow, agitation and demonstrations had intensified after the Wall crumbled. To Brent Scowcroft, warily watching from the White House, "the wave of popular demand for change had slammed into one of the most immovable regimes of the Warsaw Pact and overwhelmed it. The East German government tottered. . . . The revolutions had now crossed the line from surging to overpowering."[8]

So overpowering, in fact, that Modrow was forced to schedule multiparty elections for May 1990. The mere announcement was a victory for the dissenters, and in the promised elections the Communists suffered a crushing defeat. A newly formed independent government opened negotiations with West Germany (officially the Federal Republic of Germany, or FRG) and reunification actually was declared in October 1990. Thus, one of the Soviet Union's most important foreign policy principles—the division of Germany—dating back forty-five years to the end of World War II, was demolished, not by Western armed force but by Mikhail Gorbachev's cancellation of the Brezhnev Doctrine.

None of the satellite nations was immune to change, but change took different forms in different countries—violently but incompletely, for instance, in Romania. There Nicolae Ceauşescu had maintained dictatorial Communist leadership since 1965, and had built a remarkable "cult of personality" in which, on his sixty-second birthday in 1982, the state actually had declared him "divine." As late as November 1989, just before Malta, his rule appeared to have survived the stresses of that tumultuous year. But on December 21, the "divine" Ceauşescu was rudely shouted down when he tried to speak in Bucharest. He promptly fled but was quickly captured; and on Christmas Day he and his wife were tried, sentenced to death for "genocide," and summarily executed.* Government was carried on by a coalition in which Communists remained in control; and in May 1990 their presidential candidate, Ion Iliescu, a former Politburo member, won a substantial victory. He was reelected in 1992.

Yugoslavia, after 1991, began almost literally to dissolve into separate republics, of which Slovenia and Serbia retained Communist leadership, but with elections and a nationalist program. In the Balkans, Albania, like Romania, at first appeared to have escaped the tide of change that began to flow in 1989; but after many strikes and demonstrations in that remote nation, a Democratic Party soundly defeated the Party of Labour (Communists by any other name) in 1992. But in 1997 Albania—suffering the same poor economic conditions it had resisted in 1992—reelected the former Communists, who had repudiated their Communist ideology.

In Bulgaria, too, Communists clung to at least part of their former power. The longtime leader, Todor Zhivkov, was expelled by his party colleagues in 1989, owing more to economic than to political problems. In February 1990 the party committed itself and the country to "democratic and free" elections and promised gradual economic reform.

In the Baltics, which had so concerned Gorbachev and Bush at Malta, there was nothing resembling halfhearted charge or

---

*Scowcroft believed that Chinese leaders were hardened in their attitudes by Ceauşescu's downfall. They had believed his early impregnability meant that Communism could survive liberal assault. But when Ceauşescu was thrown out and executed, Scowcroft believed, the Chinese thought "they had been right at Tiananmen . . . their only chance of survival was to be absolutely inflexible." Bush and Scowcroft, *A World Transformed*, p. 179.

retreat. In 1990 parliamentary elections, Estonia, Latvia, and Lithuania all voted clear victories for the independence parties. They left the Soviet Union in 1991, unopposed—despite Gorbachev's threats at the Malta talks.

How much reform could Gorbachev afford to allow? Did the "Sinatra Doctrine" apply not just to Eastern Europe but to the constituent republics of the Soviet Union herself?

The Communist leader's "third way" obviously was not working out. More open elections in 1989 and 1990 had stimulated nationalist movements in the republics—including the election of Boris Yeltsin as president of the Supreme Soviet in Russia. Demonstrators clamored for the removal of the Communist political monopoly from the constitution. Economic decline continued, and shortages increased.

In Russia, the biggest republic in the USSR, Yeltsin, an expelled former Communist and a critic of Gorbachev, called for Russian control over the Russian economy. In another of the republics, the Ukraine, leaders sought the recall of Ukrainian forces from the Soviet military. Beset by both reformers and conservatives, Gorbachev vainly tried to maintain his middle course and keep intact the Soviet Union, to which he had devoted much of his life. But his popularity and political standing were bottoming out; he was blamed for the breakup of the empire, for the reunification of Germany, for having "disarmed" the Soviet Union—and for ineffective halfway measures of reform at home. His foreign minister, Eduard Shevardnadze of Georgia, resigned, warning that "a dictatorship is coming."

Shevardnadze apparently feared that the old hard-liners would regain control. In 1991 they tried, staging a brief coup and imposing house arrest on Gorbachev while he was on vacation in the Crimea. He had a telephone, however, and used it freely to raise the alarm. Many Soviet citizens took to the streets to protest the coup; they had thought such a Third World tactic could not succeed in their powerful country. Yeltsin bravely faced down tanks and troops to call for resistance. An estimated seventy thousand Muscovites responded, surrounding and protecting the parliament building—not so much on Gorbachev's behalf as in patriotic loyalty to their country and its established government. The coup began to collapse; a day later the conspirators were arrested, and Gorbachev was released.

The attempted coup nevertheless had profound effects, not only for Gorbachev but for the USSR; it led straight to declarations of independence in several republics, and to their assumption of national sovereignty. In Russia, moreover, Yeltsin was able to order the dissolution of the Communist Party, which had done little to resist the attempt to oust Gorbachev. Thereafter, the Commonwealth of Independent States was formed by three of the former constituent republics, all of which had withdrawn from the Soviet Union.

On December 25, 1991, Mikhail Gorbachev resigned, and Boris Yeltsin moved into Gorbachev's old office in the Kremlin. The Warsaw Pact was effectively dead; the Cold War was all but over. The United States and its allies had won it without launching a missile.

On that Christmas Day, George Bush and Mikhail Gorbachev held the last conversation* between a president of the United

---

*By telephone, Gorbachev calling from Moscow.

States and a leader of the Soviet Union. Characteristically Bush assured Gorbachev that "he would be [Gorbachev's] friend always" and also that "history would treat him kindly."

> GB: At this special time of year and at this historic time, we salute you and thank you for what you have done for world peace. . . .
> MG: Thank you, George. . . . I am saying goodbye and shaking your hands. You have said to me many important things and I appreciate it.[9]

These final words of personal regard seem a strange coda to four decades of Cold War, nuclear apprehension, and almost constant political hostility between rival states—and nearly half of my life, for instance, spent in some degree of fear. Any other two men in the positions of Bush and Gorbachev on December 25, 1991, might well—perhaps should—have been less generous to each other. But *they* were there, not two others, because the Soviet Union had collapsed on *their* watch.

Gorbachev had been more nearly the mover and shaker at the time, often unintentionally; Bush had been mostly an interested—though restrained—observer. They had so conducted themselves, even in their rivalry, that their final words to each other must have come as naturally as breathing. And anyway, at least in George Bush's experience, after a spirited match winners and losers always shake hands across the net.

CHAPTER SEVEN

As TIME WENT ON, it became clearer that George Bush's un-emotional response to the dissolution of the Soviet Union and the revolt of its satellites had been a sensible, if not the most popular or exciting, policy. Bush's instinctive dislike of boasting (the "me-me-me stuff") had served him and the nation well.

At the time Bush had to take a lot of criticism: on the one hand from American conservatives who thought he should have celebrated Communist troubles—just think, some said, how Ronald Reagan would have memorialized the fall of the Berlin Wall—and on the other from liberals who thought the president should have embraced and encouraged softening attitudes in the Soviet Union. But these domestic critics could not have set off a violent response from Moscow, or a civil war within the USSR—two possibilities about which the president worried constantly and properly. Sometimes he may have exceeded his writ, as in August 1991, when in Kiev he openly advised Ukrainians not to be misled by "suicidal nationalism" into seeking independence from the Soviet Union. But on the whole Bush successfully kept to a middle course between the U.S. national interest and Gorbachev's effort to end the Cold War.

Robert Gates, the director of central intelligence in the last year of the Bush administration, before that an assistant to Brent

Scowcroft, was unrestrained in his admiration of the president's conduct:

> He did not gloat [Gates wrote]. He did not make grandiose announcements. . . . [H]e did not threaten or glower. . . . As the Communist bloc was disintegrating, it was George Bush's skilled, yet quiet, statecraft that made a revolutionary time seem so much less dangerous than it actually was.[1]

Scowcroft himself was less effusive but still approving of the policy Bush followed in response to the Communist meltdown:

> Our policy of refusing to exult over the course of events, first in Eastern Europe and then in Germany, or to talk in terms of victory for "us" and defeat for "them," helped to reassure [Gorbachev] that we looked at events not as a zero-sum game but rather as one in which there were only winners.

Scowcroft has been frank to admit, however, that luck played as large a part as did the president's instincts in forging a new Europe, one in which ancient enemies as well as recent adversaries could participate without real bitterness or recrimination—unlike the aftermath of the Versailles treaty of 1919. On the two Germanies, for instance, he conceded that the United States shared the conventional wisdom that reunification would not be possible for many years. As a result the administration had done little advance planning for what proved to be the swift joining of East and West Germany, much less for the reunited nation's inclusion in NATO: "Our reaction was perforce ad hoc rather than strategic . . . we had to scramble to get our act together."[2]

Today Bush's middle-course policy in 1989–91 is generally approved, though still disputed by some scholars. Fifteen years have passed, after all, since another superpower could rain death and destruction on a fearful America, and the emotions of the Cold War—the "long, twilight struggle" John Kennedy spoke of in his 1961 inaugural address—may seem strange and archaic to a youthful generation that never knew them.

As the 1980s turned into the 1990s, the Soviet colossus was coming apart in Europe, and the Chinese dragon apparently was taking a hard right turn in Asia. After less than a year in office, President Bush hardly needed to deal also with the less cosmic distraction of Manuel Noriega, the drug trafficker and ex-CIA informer who was also dictator of Panama. Yet Bush was scarcely home from Malta and his first meeting with Mikhail Gorbachev when he was confronted with the frustrating, seemingly endless Noriega mess—specifically, the aftermath of an unsuccessful "covert" action that Bush himself had approved:

A few weeks earlier, on October 3, 1989, a Panama Defense Force (PDF) officer, one Moises Giroldi, had staged a coup with U.S. collaboration, and actually took a surprised Noriega into custody—but only for a few hours. U.S. forces had failed to carry out a crucial part of the operation: blocking two specified roads. After these failures the United States did nothing further; the PDF rallied to free Noriega, Giroldi was tortured and killed, and George Bush suddenly found himself tarred again with the hated "wimp image" of 1988.

The failure of U.S. action, and of the coup itself—though Bush tried to deny that the United States had had anything to do with it—aroused widespread criticism in the press and in Congress. Senator Jesse Helms, Republican of North Carolina, called the Bush administration "a bunch of Keystone Kops." George Will, he of the old "lapdog" charge, weighed in again, writing that Bush's was "an unserious presidency." The chairman of the House Select Committee on Intelligence, Representative Dave McCurdy, Democrat of Oklahoma, said Bush's failure to push through the Giroldi coup "makes Jimmy Carter look like a man of resolve."

The president and administration officials responded with excuses, mostly lacking credibility. But just a month before Giroldi tried to act, Bush had said in his first nationally televised speech from the White House that "the gravest domestic threat facing our nation today is drugs." He also had called Noriega the number one public enemy of the United States. Now the inescapable fact was that Giroldi had created an opportunity to remove Noriega and strike a blow against the drug trade—but Bush and the military, after encouraging the effort, had failed to seize the moment. If the president of the United States couldn't even deal with a drug criminal in a banana republic in his own backyard, it was asked in the press and in Congress, how could he handle more important challenges and take the lead in world affairs?

Noriega had been a concern at least since he had taken power in Panama in 1983. Long before that, perhaps as far back as the Kennedy years and certainly during George Bush's brief tenure at the CIA, he had been an "asset" on the agency's payroll for an amount estimated sometimes to have risen to two hundred thousand dollars a year. The Reagan administration, particularly CIA Director William Casey, had at first encouraged him—Noriega was not a Communist and no one thought he was under

Soviet influence—but the growing drug problem in the United States eventually turned Reagan against him.* Not only was Noriega involved in drug trafficking, arms smuggling, and money laundering; he oppressed his own people and was charged with violations of American-Panamanian canal treaties.

How bad was Noriega, actually, in light of the later demonization of Iraq's Saddam Hussein? Apparently Noriega was not as oppressive as some other Latin dictators of the time, though he roughly shut down opposition rallies and manipulated ballot boxes. He had often served U.S. interests in Latin America (and thought he deserved thanks, not condemnation), he never sought weapons of mass destruction or threatened attacks on other nations, and his defenders contend that some of his shadowy activities actually may have helped along the "war on drugs." In Washington's view he was undoubtedly arrogant, crooked, and obnoxious; international monitors, including former president Carter, established conclusively that he had rigged the Panamanian elections of May 1989; and his long-ago connection with CIA director Bush, though impersonal, must have been an embarrassment to the vice president, soon to become president.

Once disenchanted with Noriega and eager to be rid of him, Ronald Reagan authorized covert operations, imposed economic sanctions, encouraged popular uprisings, supported plans for

---

*Charges persist, without evidence, that Reagan's real purpose, and later Bush's, in opposing Noriega was to reassert U.S. control of the Panama Canal. Noriega, moreover, had cooperated only minimally with the contra war against the Sandinistas in Nicaragua. The U.S.–Panama conflict also has been charged to the ancient U.S. policy of intervening in Latin countries to exert political and military control over them.

one or more coups—sometimes with U.S. funds—and tried constantly to coerce or purchase the dictator's departure from Panama. Reagan never approved a military invasion, however, even though nothing else he tried worked to get rid of Noriega; apparently he wanted to preserve the Panamanian regime and the PDF, but without Noriega.

Then, in February 1988, a Florida grand jury indicted the dictator on drug charges—an unprecedented act, if not illegal under international law (because the crimes of which Noriega was accused had been committed in Panama). Over Vice President Bush's private opposition (see chapter 4), Reagan then tried a swap: if Noriega would go away, into exile or oblivion, the Florida indictments would be quashed. That didn't work either.

In 1988 George Bush made a "war" against drugs one of his loudest presidential campaign themes—other than his attacks on Michael Dukakis. "Noriega must go," he authorized a spokesman to say soon after he had defeated Dukakis. In his inaugural address, speaking of the drug epidemic, Bush declared: "This scourge will stop." But then another covert action failed in Panama; and though former president Carter and other monitors reported that Noriega had falsified the May 1989 elections to his own advantage, this charge resulted only in more defiance from the unabashed dictator.

Through the years, mixed messages and ambiguous signals from the United States—not to mention Noriega's CIA connection—had allowed him to believe he need not really worry about U.S. military action. When, in 1989, for instance, President Bush announced a seven-point plan for Noriega's ouster—pointedly not ruling out military force—Secretary of Defense Richard

Cheney said U.S. troops would not intervene or be involved with "deciding who governs Panama." Whom was Noriega to believe?

Following the failed Giroldi coup and the consequent uproar in the United States, Noriega—as such chesty characters often do—finally overstepped himself, perhaps misled by Cheney. On December 15, 1989, Noriega had his tame legislative assembly appoint him chief of government and "maximum leader"—and in the same session declare Panama to be in a "state of war" with the United States. These actions precipitated several serious incidents—including the killing of a Marine Corps lieutenant, and U.S. retaliatory actions.

On December 17, 1989, a meeting of President Bush's principal advisers considered these provocations and incidents of disorder. Gen. Colin Powell, the new chairman of the Joint Chiefs of Staff, advocated a large-scale military intervention to destroy the PDF and the entire Noriega regime—contrary to Reagan's old policy of preserving everything but the dictator himself. Bush promptly ordered the attack Powell had outlined, later dubbed Operation Just Cause (though, in the event, international law was spurned and may have been broken).

Three days later, just after midnight on December 20, 1989, fourteen thousand American troops smashed their way into Panama, joining the thirteen thousand already stationed in the Canal Zone; at the time it was the largest U.S. military operation since the Vietnam War. Subsequent fighting and aerial bombardment caused hundreds—probably thousands—of Panamanian military and civilian deaths and did horrendous damage to Panama City and its El Chorillo district. U.S. casualties totaled a minuscule 25 killed, including two civilians, and 324 injured.

In a brief period of martial law after combat died down,
American troops also detained thousands of Panamanian civilians. After a long and fruitless search, they captured Manuel
Noriega himself, though not until January 3, 1990. He was returned to the United States for trial—another act of disputed
legality under accepted international law—and was convicted
under the Florida indictment.

Noriega is still serving, in a Miami prison, the forty-year sentence imposed on him. Perhaps not coincidentally, the new talk
about George Bush's persistent wimp image quickly died down.[3]

Operation Just Cause provoked sharp criticism in the United
States and much of the world for overkill—a bloodier outcome
than the cause seemed to warrant—and, as was only to be expected, from Latin nations deploring another military intervention by the Colossus of the North.

It had always been unrealistic, however, to expect Noriega to
step down voluntarily, or under diplomatic and economic threat.
No matter what incentives or pressures the United States employed, Noriega not only stayed in place but expanded his control
in Panama. Dictators do not easily give up personal power, and so
many nonmilitary U.S. efforts to oust Noriega probably persuaded
him that he had little cause to fear a full-scale assault; in fact, evidence suggests that he had no inkling of what was about to happen on December 20 until a few hours before Just Cause began to
explode around him. Besides, the drug business is not easy to get
out of; had he quit his position of power, a Noriega without the
PDF or a strategic position in Panama could have become an in-
stant target for the drug lords of other countries.

Bush therefore followed the only practical course—even

though Ronald Reagan had never been willing to order an invasion—to rid Panama and himself of Manuel Noriega, whether or not that course was legally or morally justified, whether or not it was overkill. On another front, however, the new president had followed Reagan's policy of friendship and assistance, including supplying arms, to the brutal regime of a more threatening dictator than Noriega had ever been—Saddam Hussein of Iraq.

In view of the war that Bush eventually organized and waged against Saddam in 1990–91, when he compared Saddam to Adolf Hitler, many Americans today may not know that Iraq had been a favored American ally during the Reagan administration, and continued to be so until well into George Bush's first term.*
In the eighties, Iraq and Iran fought a bloody and protracted war; the United States more than "tilted" toward Iraq, a nation seen as preferable to the fundamentalist Islamic regime of the Ayatollah Khomeini and his successors in revolutionary Iran. Though the Iraqis actually attacked first, in September 1980, Saddam then was considered in Washington as a barrier to Iranian penetration or conquest of pro-American states like Kuwait, Saudi Arabia, and Jordan—and ultimately Israel. Not forgotten, either, was Iran's defiant holding of American hostages in the 1970s—a long-running drama that caused many Americans to detest Iran and regard President Carter as weak and irresolute (not the least reason for his defeat by Reagan in 1980).

When the Iranians rallied, threw back the Iraqi attack, and

*In view, too, of renewed fulminations against Saddam, in 2002 and 2003, by George H. W. Bush's son, President George W. Bush, culminating in another war on Iraq, beginning in March 2003.

threatened to win the war in 1982 and 1983, putting Iraq on the defensive and endangering U.S. oil supplies, the Reagan administration came to the economic and geopolitical conclusion that an Iraqi defeat had to be prevented. Bush and Scowcroft, in a "narrative voice" section connecting their individual accounts in *A World Transformed,* claim that Reagan's decision was made "not out of preference for one of two reprehensible nations" but because the United States wanted neither side to win the war and feared that Iraq was the weaker.[4] Written long *after* the period of U.S. aid to Iraq, and after that policy's abrupt reversal in the Gulf War, this strained explanation has a ring of ex post facto apologia for what had been, it now appears, a misguided and cynical policy.[5]

It was widely believed during the 1980s war that Saddam's troops were using chemical weapons in defiance of international agreements and the Reagan administration's stated policy. Saddam's human rights record was abysmal, and in Washington he was believed to be seeking, perhaps building, nuclear weapons. Nevertheless Iraq was removed from the State Department's list of terrorist nations in order to make possible the assistance the Reagan administration had decided to provide.

Thereafter the administration supplied Baghdad with invaluable intelligence information, billions in trade credits, and an ample supply of arms—including insecticides that could be used in chemical warfare, as well as certain strains of anthrax to be used in biological warfare. Some of this aid came direct from the United States with the approval or silent acquiescence of the Reagan administration; some was allowed to be sent from, or through, other nations—while at the same time Washington was trying to enforce Operation Staunch, to stop the international sale of arms to Iran. Even when Iraqi forces used chemical war-fare against villages in northern Iraq, where local Kurds were co-operating with invading Iranians, the Reagan administration did nothing to endanger its close relations with Saddam Hussein's regime.*

Those relations had been confirmed in December 1983, when Reagan's special envoy to the Middle East, Donald Rumsfeld,† met with Saddam Hussein in Baghdad. Rumsfeld apparently made no convincing protests against Iraq's use of chemical warfare but cited that use as only one of several problems—obviously not insurmountable—for the United States in providing assistance to Iraq.

After George H. W. Bush became the forty-first president in January 1989, he reviewed but made no significant change in the Reagan policy of support for Saddam Hussein—though to a questioner at Tufts University on February 26, 2003 (ten years after he left the White House), Bush denied that his administration ever supplied arms to Iraq: "I don't think we did that." In October 1989, however, in National Security Directive (NSD) 26, he had reaffirmed U.S. strategic interests in the Gulf region and Reagan's policy. "Normal relations between the United States and Iraq [NSD 26 declared] would serve our longer term interests and promote" stability in the region.

---

*Much outrage was expressed, however, in Congress and the press. And in 2002 and 2003, the second President Bush condemned Saddam Hussein for using chemical warfare against his own people, not mentioning tacit U.S. complicity in this atrocity.

†The former secretary of defense under President Ford, Rumsfeld took that office a second time in 2003, under the second President Bush, and became a leading advocate of military action to overthrow Saddam.

Tom Wicker

Bush's ambassador to Baghdad, April Glaspie, assured Saddam in July 1990 that Bush "wanted better and deeper relations." Later, referring to Iraq's border wrangle with Kuwait, Glaspie told Saddam, "as you know, we don't take a stand on territorial disputes."*

The next month Saddam Hussein invaded Kuwait—one of the pro-American, oil-rich nations that the United States had tried to protect from Iran by supporting Iraq.

Even as Glaspie assured Saddam of continuing U.S. regard, tensions between Iraq and Kuwait had been rising—owing to a dispute within OPEC on oil production, long-standing territorial and border animosities, and Iraqi demands that Kuwait forgive its share of Baghdad's eighty-billion-dollar debt from the war with Iran. In Washington that summer, Bush's administration had reached a low point politically, owing to the breaking, on June 26, of his famous pledge: "Read my lips, no new taxes." The president was still engaged in a savage budget battle with Congress, the economy was in recession, the midterm elections were approaching, the Soviet Union and Eastern Europe were in crisis, China remained defiant, and Bush's Oval Office desk was littered with lesser problems, from Trinidad to Liberia.

On August 1, for relaxation from all this, the athletic Bush hit a bucket of golf balls on the White House lawn. He was getting a deep-heat treatment for the resulting sore shoulders when Scowcroft and Richard Haas, a Middle East specialist for the

*President Bush said criticism of this statement was unfair, as Glaspie was only using "standard State Department language that we do not take positions on the merits of a boundary dispute, but expect it to be settled peacefully." Bush and Scowcroft, *A World Transformed,* p. 311.

NSC, told him that intelligence reports suggested Saddam was about to invade Kuwait; Iraqi troops were massed on the border. An hour later Scowcroft confirmed the bad news; Iraq's forces had crossed into Kuwait (shortly after midnight on August 2, 1990, Kuwait time).

The obvious possibility was that Saudi Arabia would be next. But Saddam Hussein in control there would be unacceptable to the United States and to the West generally—owing to Saudi oil resources and to the necessity to prevent such aggression in the new order about to follow the disappearing East-West bipolar world balance between the United States and the Soviet Union.

By the day following the invasion, the Bush administration had acted to freeze Iraqi and Kuwaiti assets in the United States, before Saddam could plunder the latter. In the next few days, from hasty administration meetings in the White House and at Camp David, and one between Bush and Prime Minister Thatcher in Aspen, Colorado, plus a blizzard of telephone calls between the president and other world leaders, several prime conclusions emerged:

- Saudi Arabia had to be protected, and that would require the presence of U.S. and perhaps other foreign forces in Saudi territory—a proposition to which King Fahd's government, wary about the perceptions of other Arab nations, was at first reluctant to agree.
- Iraqi control of Kuwait through invasion and a puppet government could not be permitted—Saddam's invasion would have to be rolled back and the Kuwaiti royal family restored; any lesser "solution" would involve at least partial acceptance of aggression and would leave Iraqi forces on the Saudi border.

- The support of Mikhail Gorbachev and the battered but still standing Soviet Union would be necessary if U.S. efforts to forestall Saddam were to succeed. The Soviets had veto power in the UN Security Council and had been for years Iraq's principal military and economic sponsors. If they now lined up *against* Saddam Hussein, the possibility of isolating him and organizing a powerful coalition to reverse his aggression would become real.
- The general approval of the Arab world was necessary to the anti-Saddam effort. Other Middle East nations should be cautioned not to accept, out of fear, his aggression or his puppet government in Kuwait, and they should not be given reason to believe that the United States and the West were unfairly singling out Iraq or acting on behalf of Israel.

On Saturday, August 4, 1990, Secretary of Defense Richard Cheney; Colin Powell, chairman of the Joint Chiefs of Staff; and Gen. Norman Schwarzkopf, the commander in chief of Central Command (responsible for military activities in the Gulf region), laid out preliminary military plans for the defense of Saudi Arabia and, perhaps ultimately, the ejection of Iraq from Kuwait. They assured the president that forces and equipment were available to do the job, though it would take time to get them all in place.

Saudi hesitations were unofficially removed when the president assured Fahd that "the security of Saudi Arabia was vital—basically fundamental—to US interests and really to the interests of the Western world." As for Saudi fears that the United States would falter in its determination to fend off Saddam, Bush gave the king his "solemn word" that "once we are there, we will stay until we are asked to leave."[6] Saudi acceptance of U.S. forces—soon confirmed by Fahd to a U.S. mission headed by Cheney and Schwarzkopf—went a long way toward bringing most other Arab nations into the emerging coalition against Iraq.

Secretary of State James Baker, working with Soviet Foreign Minister Shevardnadze in Moscow, was able to produce a joint U.S.–Soviet declaration condemning the invasion of Kuwait.* Aside from signaling that Iraq's primary supporter had turned against Saddam, as Scowcroft noted in Washington: "it dramatically put the two superpowers on the same side of a major crisis for the first time since the Cold War began."[7] Moreover, the declaration would greatly advance the possibility of a solid bloc of nations supporting UN resolutions and erecting economic sanctions against Iraq.

Thus armed, and reasonably sure of cooperation from the foreign leaders he had consulted—many of whom he had known personally since his days as ambassador to the UN—Bush returned from Camp David to Washington on Sunday, August 5. The press awaited him on the White House lawn, and in answer to questions, he said: "I view very seriously our determination to reverse this awful aggression. And please believe me, there are an awful lot of countries that are in total accord with what I've just said . . . we will be working with them all for collective action. This will not stand, this aggression against Kuwait."

Watching television in Quarters Six at Fort Meyer in Virginia, Colin Powell sat up straight when he heard those words.

---

*Not all Soviet leaders approved the declaration, pushed primarily by Shevardnadze without much help from Gorbachev. Bush and Scowcroft, *A World Transformed*, p. 326.

"Had the President just committed the United States to liberating Kuwait?" he asked himself. Powell turned off the television and began to consult a map, thinking, "I might have just received a new mission."[8]

August 1–5, 1990, may well have justified—if any justification is needed—George Bush's lifelong pursuit of friendships. From the UN, from China, from his tenure at the CIA, and from his eight years as vice president—flying tirelessly to all those funerals, representing the United States on countless foreign occasions—Bush had acquired what probably was a matchless personal acquaintance with other national leaders, relationships indispensable to his diplomacy in building "collective action" against Saddam Hussein.

It was not mere exposure or pro forma handshakes that had made him so many friends. George Bush had a natural gift for friendship, a sunny disposition, an optimistic outlook, a sympathetic understanding of other people's problems and concerns, a genuine interest in those he dealt with. He had been taught from birth to be a team player, not to boast or bully, to respect opponents as well as colleagues, to win modestly and to lose gracefully (but to value winning and hate losing, as in his uncharacteristically savage 1988 presidential race, when his highest ambition was at stake).

So when Bush picked up the Oval Office telephone to call this president or that prime minister, the occasional general or business tycoon, perhaps a dictator or a prince of the blood, whoever was on the other end of the conversation was not listening awestruck or resentful to just the powerful president of the United States, the man with his finger on the button and the bomb at his disposal. He or she also was hearing the voice of a personal friend, at least that of a friendly and likable man—the kind of guy, Bush himself might have said, with whom you could relax, put your feet up on the desk, share the latest jokes, and knock back a couple of beers.

Even on the sticky but crucial business of war, George Bush was a hard man to resist. Following Saddam's plunge into Kuwait, few other world leaders did resist him, or the pull of their own interests. Most nations wanted to play on the American, not the Iraqi, side; most wanted aggression to be punished, at least halted, not rewarded; many were naturally concerned for their supply of Middle East oil—points Bush could hardly fail to make.

In the first week after the invasion, the UN Security Council imposed an economic embargo on Iraq; Saddam responded by "annexing" Kuwait. Clearly he would not back off quickly. But in that same first week, mainly owing to Bush's prodding, a large international coalition began to form, with the prime intent of protecting Saudi Arabia and liberating Kuwait.

Eventually the United States was to send more than four hundred thousand troops to Saudi Arabia—the first loaded C-141 taking off from the Charleston, South Carolina, Air Force Base on August 7. According to an Internet history of the war, more than two hundred thousand others were supplied by Saudi Arabia itself, the United Kingdom, France, Kuwait, Egypt, Senegal, Niger, Mexico, Bangladesh, Pakistan, the United Arab Emirates, Qatar, Oman, and Bahrein. Ships, medical units, and air forces came from Canada, Italy, Argentina, Australia, Belgium, Denmark, Greece, Norway, Spain, Portugal, Czechoslovakia, New Zealand, the Netherlands, Poland, and South Korea. Turkey provided air bases; Germany and Japan gave financial support.[9]

Probably no other such worldwide group of nations ever had been put together for any purpose—certainly not for war or to repel aggression.

Organizing the coalition, of course, was not the same as putting an army in the field, equipped to take on Iraq—which at that time was ranked the world's fourth largest military power. Saddam had deployed nearly half a million men with thousands of tanks and artillery pieces in and around Kuwait; and his forces had eight years of combat experience in the war against Iran. As it turned out, however, the Iraqis had the wrong kind of experience for fighting the mobile war that impended; this was not at first realized by either side.

Combining all the coalition troops into a single army, ready and able to fight, with effective battle plans and the equipment to carry them out, was the first, perhaps the most difficult, task. Before a shot was fired in anger, the logistics of getting hundreds of thousands of men safely into a relatively backward country, building the bases and airfields to accommodate them, feeding and arming them, maintaining their morale far from home and in furnacelike heat, was a daunting task. It fell mostly to the Pentagon and to General Schwarzkopf in the field, as the United States naturally took the military as well as the diplomatic lead.

On August 15, two weeks into the mobilization, Joint Chiefs Chairman Powell could tell President Bush that as of that day, nearly thirty thousand American troops had been transported eight thousand miles, into Saudi Arabia—almost enough to *deter* an Iraqi attack, if that's what Saddam had in mind. By December, Powell estimated, one hundred eighty-four thousand troops would be deployed in the desert, enough to *defend* Saudi Arabia if Saddam had not been deterred from attack. But to reach that level, Bush would have to call out the reserves—a disruptive action Americans might not welcome. If international sanctions failed to cause Saddam to withdraw from Kuwait, and if Bush then wanted an *offensive* force to drive out the invaders, even more troops would be needed—and even more than that if, after Kuwait had been freed, Iraq itself was to be conquered.[10]

Bush still had not made it clear, nor had he decided in his own mind, whether the mammoth operation, called Desert Shield, was to remain defensive or would go on to free Kuwait (that operation would be called Desert Storm), or would then try to destroy Saddam Hussein's regime. All were separate missions, though building on one another. This ambiguity of objectives troubled military leaders, particularly Powell and Schwarzkopf. The latter, as commander on the scene, also had to deal with the stresses and strains of organizing and leading a multinational force and dealing with its back-home leaders—much the same sort of "alliance politics" that Dwight Eisenhower was celebrated for having successfully practiced in World War II.

Numerous cultural problems arose from the clash of western customs with Islamic law and attitudes. Saudi Arabia wanted no Bibles on its territory, for instance, though U.S. religious groups were flooding the Pentagon with gift Bibles for the troops. The Saudis wanted no religious services for Jewish servicemen, no alcohol for anybody, and no crucifixes. American servicewomen driving military vehicles baffled and angered Saudi men, and caused some defiant Saudi women to start driving themselves, only to be arrested for violating Islamic law. All these problems were gradually worked out, not without ingenuity on both sides; the Bibles, for example, were shipped directly into Western military bases, while Saudi customs officials looked the other way.

At first, too, Saudi Arabia ruled that no foreign reporters would be allowed to cover the military buildup. The Americans, in particular, with their tradition of press freedom, could not accept this restriction, and protested strongly; after all, though it was the Saudis' country, the United States and the coalition were defending it. Eventually the Saudis relented and, ultimately, about twenty-five hundred correspondents were accredited. Paradoxically, this influx made it easier for the military to control the news; press "pools" had to be organized, the movements of other reporters restricted, and the use of TV satellites rationed.

In Washington, the Pentagon had to overcome Bush's and the general American predilection for airpower—which, it was too easily assumed, could win the victory at a low price in casualties. The air force chief of staff, Michael Dugan, was summarily relieved by Defense Secretary Cheney, with Bush's approval, for making too many and too bold claims for the efficacy of airpower, hence raising expectations for a quick and easy war. Historically air attack had never substituted successfully for troops on the ground, except in limited cases. Cheney and Powell not only considered Dugan insubordinate; they thought it necessary for the American people—including George H. W. Bush—to understand that the desert war would be no picnic of "surgical" air strikes.[11]

On October 30, Bush made the crucial decision for which the military had been hankering: Sanctions, he concluded, would take too long to force Saddam out of Kuwait, if they ever did; so an army twice the size of the already-deployed defense force would be created to *drive* him out, if he had not withdrawn by a specified date. After the November 8 midterm elections—in which Bush's broken no-new-taxes pledge led to Republican political losses—the president made his decision public: Another two hundred thousand troops would go to Saudi Arabia to give Schwarzkopf and the coalition the offensive capacity to recapture Kuwait.

This announcement was not without political risk; it set off a debate in the country not unlike the divisions caused, years earlier, by the war in Vietnam. Was war on Iraq, instead of the mere defense of Saudi Arabia, the proper policy? And even if it was, did the president have the authority to order such an operation without a congressional declaration of war? Vociferous arguments were advanced on both sides of each question; for instance, Sam Nunn of Georgia, the powerful Democrat who chaired the Senate Armed Services Committee, strongly favored waiting for sanctions to become effective enough to force Saddam to withdraw from Kuwait. The issue, however, never became precisely one of Republicans versus Democrats; some of both were to be found on either side.

Passage of Resolution 678 by the UN Security Council on November 29 provided vital approval for the coalition and for Bush's policy of actively freeing Kuwait. The resolution authorized the use of "all necessary means"—a phrase obviously including military force—to remove Iraqi forces from Kuwait, if they had not been voluntarily withdrawn by January 15, 1991. The Soviet Union, which could have vetoed the resolution, instead cooperated in devising language that made passage possible. Only Cuba and Yemen voted no, though China abstained. Crucially, however, the resolution provided only for the liberation of Kuwait—not for a further attack on Iraq.

Powell defended this restriction more realistically than Bush and Scowcroft had described the period of U.S. aid to Iraq *before* its invasion of Kuwait:

> We wanted Iraq to continue as a threat and a counterweight to Iran. . . . [D]ismembering Iraq, conquering Baghdad, or changing the Iraqi form of government [was never] seriously considered. . . . What we hoped for frankly, in a postwar Gulf region was an Iraq still standing, with Saddam overthrown.[12]

The defiant Saddam, who could have withdrawn from Kuwait with some modicum of excuse at several points during the autumn of 1990—for instance, after the passage of Resolution 678 by the Security Council—had steadfastly refused to do so, despite the enormous buildup of forces against him. On January 6, nine days before the January 15 UN deadline, his forces still stood fast in Kuwait behind what appeared to be formidable defensive works (including oil-filled ditches to be set afire when an attack was launched by the coalition). That day, Bush and his military advisers decided to attack at three o'clock in the morning of January 17, Saudi time—barring an Iraqi withdrawal they no longer wanted, if they ever had, since that would leave Saddam, in effect, unpunished for his aggression. Nor did they believe the dictator *would* withdraw.

The decision to attack was not publicly announced, and on January 9, in Washington, Congress finally settled at least part of the much-debated issue of what could be done about Kuwait. The House voted 250 to 183, and the Senate by a narrower 52 to 47, to authorize military action if the president had exhausted all efforts to cause Iraq to obey UN demands that it withdraw from

Kuwait.* This more nearly resembled the "Tonkin Gulf resolution" than it did a declaration of war, and it did not settle the ultimate question of the president's authority as commander in chief of the armed forces: did the Constitution empower him to take the nation into a war other than to repel an attack on the United States? That deeper question might have been raised if Congress had refused to approve the war, and if Bush then had ordered it on his own. As it was, the matter was left to be argued again a decade later, this time between some members of Congress and Bush's son, President George W. Bush—once more on the question of a war against Saddam Hussein and Iraq, but a very different war.

In 1991, however, with both the UN and Congress behind him, the polls showing general public support, the military buildup in Saudi Arabia complete, and both Arabs and the Soviets onboard, George Bush thought he had all the authority he needed. On the evening of January 16, 1991, in Washington (the morning of January 17 in the Middle East), Schwarzkopf launched a shattering air attack, one of the greatest the world had ever seen, designed particularly to destroy Iraq's command, control, and transportation systems, to knock out its air defenses—and to pulverize many of its troops on the ground in Kuwait.

The Gulf War had begun, and viewers around the world could watch the spectacular opening moves on television—a bravura show of smart bombs, guided missiles, screaming planes, fiery

*In *My American Journey* (p. 489), Colin Powell implies at several points that Bush was prepared to go to war even if he did not win congressional approval. For instance: "I also knew that whatever Congress decided, Bush was not going to back down."

tracers, and columns of black smoke across the sky. I watched it all from a hospital bed to which I was temporarily confined in New York; what I saw on the screen suspended above me seemed rather like a fireworks display or something in a video arcade—until I realized that it was *war*, that death and destruction actually were exploding across the desert.

On the second night of the air war, Saddam struck back—though, as it turned out, not as powerfully as both sides had expected. Playing one of the most feared cards in his deck, Saddam launched seven Scud missiles into Israel. At first it was believed in Washington that some of them carried nerve gas warheads; soon, however, that was known to be false, and it was also learned that little damage had been done, with no one killed. The main problem, anyway, was not the Scuds themselves; it was to keep Israel from retaliating.

Naturally the Israeli government wanted to protect its citizens; after this first assault, Defense Minister Moshe Arens proposed to make an air, ground, or missile attack into western Iraq to find and destroy Scud launch sites. If he did any of this, especially if successfully, Israel would become a part of the coalition—which would immediately cause Arab members to depart or, in the case of Saudi Arabia, to close some or all of its territory to coalition forces. Arab nations flatly refused to fight in harness with Israel; so if the coalition was to be held together, Israel had to be persuaded to forgo retaliation for the Scuds.

After pressing telephone calls from Bush, Prime Minister Yitzhak Shamir—at considerable political risk to himself and his government—decided to hold off Arens's proposed assault into Iraq, as well as any other direct response. In return Schwarzkopf diverted more air-combat missions to destroying Scuds, special-operations troops were sent into Iraq to destroy launching sites, and the United States sent more Patriot antimissile missiles to help shield Israeli cities. Shamir, in "one of his finest moments," violated the established Israeli rule always to respond to terrorist attacks, and in that controversial way proved himself "a strong, stalwart ally"[13] of the United States and the coalition.

Six weeks later, on February 27, Saudi time, Saddam having spurned a last-ditch Soviet peace initiative,* the full juggernaut of Desert Storm was set in motion. U.S. Marines, a U.S. Army tank brigade, and a host of coalition troops surged into Kuwait, beginning four days of the most decisive military action since the blitzkrieg Battle of France in 1941.

---

*One of Mikhail Gorbachev's last appearances as an active force on the world stage.

CHAPTER EIGHT

In advance of Desert Storm, the Pentagon had ordered fifteen thousand body bags—a grim reminder of the casualties of Vietnam and earlier wars. Pressed by Secretary Cheney for his casualty estimate before the Gulf operation, a reluctant General Schwarzkopf finally put it at five thousand. Colin Powell, knowing there would be no World War I–style waves of infantry charging entrenched defenders—the Gulf battle plan rested on a mobile, armored swing around the Iraqis' western flank—went even lower, to three thousand killed, wounded, and missing.[1] But when the fighting was suspended at 8 a.m., February 28 in the Middle East, U.S. casualties actually totaled 148 killed in action and 458 wounded[2]—an almost miraculously low cost,* as surprising as the speed and ease of the coalition victory.

Perhaps the weeks of intense aerial bombardment that preceded the ground operations demoralized the Iraqis. The mobility and speed of the attack were bewildering for troops experienced mostly in the more static, though severe, Iran-Iraq fighting of the eighties. Undoubtedly, the aggressiveness, the high morale, and the high-tech equipment of the attackers overwhelmed defenders. Coalition planning and execution were superior too.

*Including eleven women's deaths in combat. Nonhostile actions accounted for 121 deaths. Nearly a third of the combat deaths, to the Pentagon's shock, were caused by "friendly fire."

For whatever reason, probably all of the above, the Iraqis were routed—there's no other word for it.[3] The "mother of battles" Saddam had predicted never materialized. Even prepared Iraqi defenses crumbled quickly. Supposedly tough and dedicated Iraqi troops surrendered in droves—10,000 in the first twenty-four hours of ground combat; 38,000 in two days; more than 60,000 in three. The flanking maneuver soon cut off thousands of Iraqi troops from a northward escape to their own country. Kuwait City was quickly surrounded, then liberated. Within forty-eight hours, twenty-seven of forty-two Iraqi divisions in the war zone were destroyed as fighting units. The highway from Kuwait City to Basra in Iraq—the so-called Highway of Death—was an open target for coalition planes, a bloody river of Iraqi soldiers on the run, and an elongated trash pile of wrecked and burning Iraqi vehicles.

In view of this smashing victory, with Cheney, Powell, and Schwarzkopf in agreement, Bush in consultation with some of his coalition partners decided to "suspend" operations—leaving open the threat of resumption—at the end of four days of remarkably successful combat. There would be no conquest of Iraq; the regime of Saddam Hussein, wounded and humiliated though it was, would remain intact. This decision was highly controversial, because Schwarzkopf's forces plainly could have swept on into Baghdad and beyond.* Nevertheless several strong reasons caused Bush to suspend operations.

*The farther coalition forces advanced beyond Kuwait into Iraq, however, the more Iraqi resistance might stiffen, since not all Iraq's army had been in the war zone. Saddam might have chosen to order a last-ditch, street-by-street, house-to-house fight in Baghdad and other cities. Even in fleeing from Kuwait, his armies had followed a sort of scorched-earth policy, setting Kuwaiti oil fields afire.

First and foremost, of course, and with startling rapidity, the mission of an international force, acting in the name of the United Nations, had been accomplished: Kuwait had been liberated, and all internationally authorized military objectives had been met. From a purely American point of view, even the possibility of "another Vietnam"—a long and lingering war with ever-declining public support—had been avoided. And the Bush administration wanted Iraq, even if badly weakened, to be preserved as a bulwark against Iran.

From an international perspective, few coalition member states wanted Iraq invaded and conquered, or a new regime imposed on it—particularly given the limitation of Resolution 678. Arab states, in particular, having helped save Saudi Arabia and redeem Kuwait, had no desire to demolish another Arab nation. The Saudis wanted to prevent a Shi'ite regime from breaking away from Iraq and establishing itself in the south, on the Saudi border. Similarly Turkey shrank from the idea of Kurds setting up a breakaway state in the north.* Stability in the Middle East, and for U.S. and Western oil supplies, would not be enhanced by an Iraq torn into separate Shi'ite, Sunni, and Kurdish enclaves.

If Iraq were to be conquered, moreover, and Saddam overthrown or thrown out, the United States might have no option but to enter into a long and difficult occupation of a war-destroyed land,† amid a surrounding sea of more or less hostile

---

*In the immediate postwar period, both Shi'ites and Kurds did revolt against Iraq, without U.S. help. Saddam Hussein subdued both uprisings with relative ease, helped greatly by Schwartzkopf's decision that the Iraqi leader could continue to use his helicopters.

†How difficult it could have been became clear in 2003, after the second U.S.–Iraq war, when guerrilla-type combat caused many U.S. casualties.

Arab countries. The American public probably would have no more enthusiasm for that difficult and expensive undertaking than it had for the idea of a long, bloody war for no obvious U.S. interest. Nor would such an occupation necessarily succeed in rebuilding an Iraq more cooperative with the West. Besides, in 1991, both the administration and Arab states wanted U.S. forces out of the Middle East as soon as possible.[4] And what effect occupation might have on overall Islamic attitudes toward the United States and the West also had to be considered (a decade before September 11, 2001).[5]

So the decision was made to suspend operations, and Saddam Hussein stayed in power, his regime battered but intact. Scowcroft and Bush explained what they saw as the most important reason:

> Apprehending him was probably impossible. . . . We would have been forced to occupy Baghdad and, in effect, rule Iraq. Going in and occupying Iraq, thus unilaterally exceeding the United Nations mandate, would have destroyed the precedent of international response to aggression that we hoped to establish. Had we gone the invasion route, the United States could conceivably still be an occupying power in a bitterly hostile land.[6]

The early end to combat nevertheless seemed premature to many critics. As still another war with Iraq became a real possibility under a second President Bush in 2002 and 2003, the first President Bush was still being queried—more than ten years after the fact—about the Gulf War's aftermath in 1991. When he lectured at Tufts University on February 26, 2003, a student asked him directly:

Q.: Mr. President, why is it that you elected not to follow through with support for the Kurdish and Shi'ite uprisings in Iraq following the first Gulf War? . . . Is this a decision you regret?

A.: Well, it wasn't a decision really . . . if there's a perception that we said, "You go rise up and we'll help you," that's an erroneous perception. I did say, "I'd like to see the Iraqi people take care of their own problems," because frankly, I and most other leaders . . . felt that the people from within would take care of Hussein. That he couldn't exist, you see. So, I was wrong in that.

But he was not wrong, he went on, in deciding not "to continue the battle" or in refusing to take "military action that might destabilize Iraq in the center."

Despite these sour notes about the ending of an otherwise satisfying war, American troops came home to wild public cheers, in sharp contrast to the chill welcome returning Vietnam veterans had encountered only a few years earlier. Cheney, Powell, and Schwarzkopf were accorded the peculiarly American honor of a Broadway ticker-tape parade.

As for George H. W. Bush, the commander in chief of Desert Shield and Desert Storm, who had vowed that Saddam's aggression "will not stand," whose diplomacy had envisioned, then organized the coalition, whose leadership had afforded his military aides everything they needed to equip its forces for war—for President Bush, victory in the Gulf War meant the highest approval rating (91 percent according to *USA Today,* 90 in a *Washington Post*/ABC News poll) ever accorded a president.

Who could believe that a second term for him was not a sure thing?

Not George Bush. And not most of the Democrats "mentioned" for their party's presidential nomination in 1992. They, and the few conservative Republicans who in other circumstances might have challenged Bush on his broken pledge not to raise taxes, took a quick look at those poll numbers and decided that 1996 or an even later year might be more promising. For a while it looked as if George Bush, the former wimp, might in 1992 be given a free ride by serious challengers from either party (as he had been reelected to the House without opposition in 1968).

Democrats and most of the press were overlooking two factors. First, those astronomical poll figures were inflated, not by chicanery on anyone's part but because they resulted from overheated, war-induced "sunshine patriotism"—the well-established national pattern that when any president sends "our boys" into battle, particularly if for an apparently noble cause, Americans tend to "rally round the flag" *and* the president. In the Gulf a smashing victory had been achieved in a worthy cause, over a villainous dictator Bush had compared to Hitler, after a quick, high-tech war visible on television, and with few casualties.

The second, less transient factor being overlooked was creeping but relentless data pointing toward an economic recession, with poll respondents in increasing numbers saying the nation was "on the wrong track." Even as Desert Shield was being mobilized, the Federal Reserve cut interest rates twice in three weeks; Chairman Alan Greenspan conceded (but the administration denied) that a "meaningful downturn" in the economy was evident in October 1990.

As the air war began in January 1991, unemployment edged up to 6.1 percent. The index of leading economic indicators slid steadily downhill, and unemployment rose to 6.2, to 6.5, then 6.8. Briefly the economy seemed to revive—to administration huzzahs—but unemployment leaped up again to 7 percent for June 1991. Nor was the business sector confidently driving ahead in the war years; what, for instance, was going to happen to oil prices?

Actually the eight years of Reaganomics, mostly continued in Bush's term, had produced a dark underside to an economy booming since 1982. The boom, in fact, had not treated all alike—the rich got richer, the poor got poorer. By 1990 the wealthiest 1 percent of the population owned 40 percent of the national wealth—the highest proportion since the 1920s.

In 1980 the lowest 20 percent of income earners had had 5.2 percent of aggregate national income; by 1992 that group's share of national income had fallen to 4.4 percent. In the same period, the richest 20 percent had *increased* their share from 41.5 to 44.6 percent of the economic pie. (These figures represent constant 1992 dollars.)

Tax cuts, for one thing, had caused the rich to prosper. From 1946 to 1963 top-bracket taxpayers had paid at the marginal rate of 88 percent; by 1988 that was down to 28 percent. In other ways, too, Reagan-Bush policies had favored the affluent; the rise in defense spending (from 23 to 28 percent in the same seven years), for instance, had gone mostly to owners and professionals in the military-industrial complex, not to "grunts" in the ranks or to workingmen.

For nine years, eight under Reagan and in the first Bush year, the minimum wage had been frozen; that meant, as inflation rose, that minimum-wage workers effectively suffered a pay cut every year. All in all the poorest tenth of the population suffered a decline of 11.8 percent in average after-tax income from 1977 to 1990 ($4,277 down to $3,805), while the top tenth *rose* from $111,100 to $133,200 (a 19.9 percent increase) and the top 1 percent leaped from $319,100 to $463,800 (a *45.4 percent* increase).

There can be little doubt that a major factor in the recession of 1991–92 was a decline in the ability of the great mass of consumers to spend money—after all, they had less to spend. In the years 1980–89 the total wages of those who earned less than $50,000 a year (about 85 percent of all Americans) increased at an average of 2 percent annually, a rate *lower* than that of inflation. They actually were losing money.

No wonder, then, that despite Desert Storm, George Bush's reelection campaign was heading into another kind of storm— not only a declining economy but the anger and resentment of its victims. Who wouldn't resent it if, after a hard day's work at the factory, one learned that one's chief executive had been paid 130 times as much for his no doubt valuable leadership. But *that* valuable?

Even when Congress passed legislation to extend unemployment benefits beyond twenty-six weeks, the president—constrained by a huge federal deficit and proclaiming "I won't bust the budget"—refused to make the declaration needed to release the $5.8 billion required. Instead he called for a cut in the capital gains tax, not a real concern to an unemployed shoemaker in New Hampshire. And when Congress passed the extended-benefits legislation a second time, Bush vetoed it.

Though economic trouble almost invariably means political trouble for those in power, Bush did not seem to be concerned.

By August 1991, when the victory glow from Desert Storm inevitably was fading, the president still had not started the necessary planning and organizing for a reelection campaign in 1992; nor had he shown special concern over the economic slippage his administration continued to doubt or deny.

He seemed confident, instead, that he would be reelected easily, on the basis of Desert Storm and the end of the Cold War. Why not? The only Democratic candidate in the field against him was former senator Paul Tsongas, not particularly impressive as another "Greek from Massachusetts," evoking memories of Michael Dukakis. Tsongas claimed to have survived the cancer that had ended his Senate career, but not everyone believed that "survived" meant "cured."

Senator Albert Gore of Tennessee, House Majority Leader Richard Gephardt, and the aggressive Jesse Jackson, all presidential candidates in 1988, showed no intent to run in 1992 (and none of them did). Nor had other Democratic big names—Senators Sam Nunn of Georgia, George Mitchell of Maine, Bill Bradley of New Jersey—entered the 1992 race, or shown serious interest in doing so. Governor Mario Cuomo of New York was a mystery, as usual; and the only Democrats who appeared likely to run were relatively minor figures like Senators Tom Harkin of Iowa, Bob Kerrey of Nebraska, and Jay Rockefeller of West Virginia, together with Governors Douglas Wilder of Virginia (the first black governor of any state) and Bill Clinton of Arkansas.

As 1991 moved along, Saddam again caused trouble, putting down the Kurds and other dissident elements, and violating the "no-fly" zones established by the coalition; Bush was criticized mildly for not intervening. The coup against Gorbachev came and quickly went, followed by the dissolution of the Soviet Union, the rise of Boris Yeltsin, and another arms reduction agreement. The president's appointment of Clarence Thomas to the Supreme Court pleased conservatives—who cheered the idea of a conservative black who would push the Court rightward as a replacement for the revered liberal, Thurgood Marshall. But women were angered after a black woman, law professor Anita Hill, accused Thomas of sexual harassment and was sternly interrogated by an all-male Judiciary Committee. To no one's surprise Thomas was confirmed anyway by a heavily male Senate.

At the end of the year Bush was embarrassed by the forced resignation of his chief of staff, John Sununu, the abrasive former governor of New Hampshire, who had made too free with government aircraft, using them frequently for personal trips.* Bush suffered another setback when Lee Atwater, an architect of the 1988 demolition of Dukakis, died of a brain tumor in March 1991. Bush *needed* someone like Atwater to get his campaign moving.

The most jarring note of the year came from Pennsylvania, where a virtually unknown Democrat, Harris Wofford—pounding on economic themes and the need for a national health care plan—upset former Republican governor Richard Thornburgh in a special election for the U.S. Senate. Less spectacular but constant was the national derision of Vice President Quayle, who had been saddled with the reputation of being a lightweight ever since

---

*"All I know," Senator Bob Dole remarked about this development, "is that every time I go into Sununu's office, a voice says, 'Make sure your seat back is upright and your tray table is locked into place.'" Or so I remember Dole's response.

his surprise selection and stumbling performance in 1988. National unease at the thought that Quayle was only "a heartbeat" from the presidency was heightened when Bush was diagnosed as suffering from Graves' disease (an affliction that could be controlled by medication). Surely, some insisted, Bush wouldn't put Quayle on the 1992 ticket when he could make a more reassuring choice—say, Colin Powell.

After Labor Day 1991, with Bush still showing little interest in the forthcoming election and not much more in the floundering economy, five more Democrats—none considered major leaguers, all encouraged by the reticence of supposed sluggers like Nunn, Bradley, and Cuomo—decided that maybe 1992 would be a promising year after all. The lonely candidacy of Paul Tsongas was joined by those of Senators Kerry and Harkin, Governors Clinton and Wilder, and the unclassifiable Jerry Brown, formerly "Governor Moonbeam" of California, twice previously a presidential candidate and—in many conventional politicians' eyes—a full-time "flake."

None of these hopefuls much impressed the electorate, and certainly not President Bush. Wilder quickly dropped out, finding candidacy and governing Virginia too hard to combine—not to mention the handicap of his race. Harkin soon looked too much like a traditional Democratic liberal in the McGovern-Mondale loser's mode (though Harkin was conceded the Democratic caucuses in Iowa, his home state). Clinton—considered by other governors as a star but not well known to the national public—began to look like the pick of the litter after he won a "beauty contest" straw vote in Florida in December 1991.

That month, however, a more serious challenge to the president developed within his own party: The flamboyant Patrick Buchanan formally entered the New Hampshire Republican primary. Neither Bush nor his political advisers—by the end of 1991 a group frustrated by the president's campaign inactivity— at first recognized Buchanan as a serious challenger. Nor did anyone think he was likely to be elected president. In fact, however, better than any of the Democrats, because he lacked the partisan overtones they could not avoid, Buchanan could develop in a Republican primary the case against Bush—not just the conservative case of "betrayal" on taxes but the broader argument that while the president was triumphing abroad, his constituents were suffering at home.

Pat Buchanan, a newspaper and television commentator, had never held other than staff political office but—curiously, in both the news and the political arenas—was also a prominent Republican leader with credentials dating back to Richard Nixon. An established conservative voice, a Roman Catholic particularly opposed to abortion, Buchanan like other conservatives had been outraged when Bush broke his read-my-lips promise not to raise taxes; but he also—like most Democrats—had been intimidated politically by the victorious war president with his astronomical approval ratings (still in the seventies, nearly a year after the end of Desert Storm).

After a long struggle, Bush accepted and signed the congressional Democrats' Civil Rights Act of 1991—falsely calling it a "quota bill," as he had in 1990 when he vetoed virtually the same legislation. Buchanan's easily aroused anger flared again. In one of his commentaries he called Bush's decision to sign a "betrayal"—which it was, from the conservative point of view, and one that came only a year after the more obvious betrayal of the no-new-taxes pledge. Well aware of Wofford's upset victory in Pennsylvania, Buchanan knew—as Bush seemed not to realize—that New Hampshire and much of the country were hurting economically; and even before he entered the primary against the president, he had the encouragement of the state's most powerful newspaper, the almost hysterically conservative *Manchester Union-Leader*.

New Hampshire is a state, too, where incumbent presidents and front-runners of both parties often have risked being upset—as were Truman and Taft in 1952. In 1968 Lyndon Johnson literally won the Democratic primary but was forced out of the general election race by Eugene McCarthy's strong showing. President Ford had won New Hampshire by only a point over Ronald Reagan in 1976, and Walter Mondale had lost it to Gary Hart in 1984. In 1980, of course, it had been in New Hampshire that Reagan derailed George Bush's first presidential bid.

So when Buchanan entered the 1992 Republican primary in New Hampshire, he could hope for a good showing, like McCarthy's a quarter century earlier; but he was too experienced in politics to think that renomination could easily be denied an incumbent president. Once in, however, he had little to lose; so he hit Bush hard and often on the broken no-tax pledge and on the signing of the "quota bill." And as Buchanan moved around New Hampshire responding to that state's highly personal political style—dropping in on diners at the breakfast hour, talking to street-corner and church-basement groups, shaking hands and chatting with voters wherever he encountered them—he learned how strong were the economic woes of ordinary people, how deep was their resentment of a president who didn't seem to care, who traveled abroad a lot, and who spent much time at his luxurious estate next door in Maine—but never came to New Hampshire to listen to or learn about ordinary people's problems.

Often in extravagant language, Buchanan eagerly exploited these local concerns, and Bush's political team began to worry about the New Hampshire challenge. Bush himself rather typically could not understand why another Republican, one he had considered a friend, would run against him. But the primary campaign caused the White House and its incumbent to realize that Buchanan and New Hampshire could send Bush a damaging message—which, not incidentally, in resentful New Hampshire, was one of Pat Buchanan's campaign talking points.

In mid-January 1992 the president reluctantly visited New Hampshire and at last acknowledged that the economy was in a bad way. He offered, however, no special help for the struggling state and seemed not to be deeply concerned. For instance, as he was reading from a three-by-five card during one speech, he carelessly read right on when he came to its stage instruction: "Message: I care."

Did he really? some in the audience must have wondered.

After his return to Washington, however, Bush finally ended his lengthy opposition to extended unemployment benefits. The White House let it get out that the president would disclose an economic plan in his State of the Union message in late January, thus arousing outsize expectations. But when he delivered the speech to the usual joint session of both houses of Congress—and to the nation on TV—he said little new about the economy and his limited proposals included that familiar Republican warhorse, a cut in the capital gains tax.

The president seemed primarily to dwell on memories of the

great military victory in the Gulf War—which might actually have backfired. It was the war, after all, that had diverted his attention from the economy. And, anyway, if he could manage a war so well, why couldn't he also do something about unemployed workers in New Hampshire and elsewhere? Now that the Cold War was over, domestic policy could be the top priority. Shouldn't it be?

The president formally entered the New Hampshire primary himself on February 12, only a week before the voting. He was then being hit, as he complained, "right and left," because the remaining Democratic primary candidates—Clinton, Kerrey, Harkin, Brown, and Tsongas—all were hammering on the economy, dwelling in speeches and debates on many of the same issues Buchanan was pressing. But it was the intraparty opposition that hurt; in a diary entry on February 16, the normally unemotional Bush described Buchanan as "mean and ugly."[7]

On primary day the president prevailed by 53 to 37 percent for Buchanan, a little better margin than polls had predicted. The insurgent had not scored as well as exit polls at first had erroneously predicted, but he and his 37 percent had indeed sent the president a stinging message: *We're hurting, and it's your fault.* In those same exit polls, moreover, that message was deafeningly amplified: Few Republicans cited victory in the Gulf War as a reason for voting as they had, but half said the economy was the prime influence on their votes.

The worst news for the president—though he probably didn't realize it—came from voters in the *Democratic* primary. They allowed the political "comeback" and survival, despite nearly fatal charges against him, of the personable young governor of Arkansas, Bill Clinton.

Clinton did not win the New Hampshire Democratic primary; he finished second, with 25 percent of the vote against 33 for Paul Tsongas, five others trailing badly (including Cuomo and Ralph Nader on write-in votes). But Tsongas was considered to have little chance outside New England, and Clinton had achieved the minimum needed to maintain his candidacy—after frantic "damage control" to counter severe late charges of "womanizing" and dodging the draft during the Vietnam War.

Clinton quickly cast himself as "the Comeback Kid," rather than reacting as just another loser. He had good reason, having overcome a "trial by fire" that, had it occurred later in the year or in other circumstances, probably would have killed his candidacy. Once he was past that early trial in New Hampshire, it would prove much harder to stop him. Bush could hardly have realized it on primary night, but if Bill Clinton was ever to be knocked out of the race in 1992, New Hampshire had been the place to do it.

Highly regarded by other governors, Clinton had won that Florida straw vote, and in various debates and candidate "cattle shows" had shown himself a natural politician and a likable campaigner. In a series of set-piece speeches, he also appeared to be a sharp student of foreign and domestic affairs. And unlike most other Democrats, Clinton was calling for a new party outlook: more in the center than on the left.

New Hampshire was the first important test for Clinton, the unofficial favorite.* He had taken a substantial lead, according to the polls, when, on January 16, the *Star*—a scandal-and-spoof

---

*In the press and among a growing number of Democratic officials and party activists.

sheet distributed mostly in supermarkets—reported with typical sensationalism that a former Arkansas state employee had alleged in a lawsuit that Clinton, as governor, had used state funds to pursue five different women, including a nightclub singer named Gennifer Flowers. The suit was old news in Arkansas, where the local press, following investigations, had found it to be vengeful and untrue; so the Clinton campaign was ready with denials from all five women. The story, nevertheless, had a certain plausibility; rumors of marital infidelity and sexual adventures had hung about Clinton for years, so heavily that he and his strategists had made an early move to dispel them.

In September 1991, they arranged for the Clintons to appear at one of the ritual Washington press breakfasts organized by Godfrey Sperling of the *Christian Science Monitor*. Clinton assured attending reporters that unspecified difficulties in his twenty-year marriage had been overcome; that he and Hillary Clinton had stuck together and loved each other. Who could doubt or question that, when Hillary sat right there at her husband's side?

This line—marriage difficulties overcome—became the standard Clinton response, a reply that he and his strategists counted on to keep his alleged "womanizing" out of the news. After the *Star* story in January, they were quickly disabused of such wishful thinking. Despite their denials, moreover, a week after its first story, the *Star* struck again, with blaring headlines and a first-person account by Gennifer Flowers of a long love affair with Governor Clinton. Her story was more or less backed by tapes she said she had made of telephone calls between them.

Campaigning that day in Claremont, New Hampshire, Clinton was besieged by the press, again denied the story, and charged that Flowers was being paid to make the accusation.* WMUR-TV in Manchester, New Hampshire, nevertheless spread the chaotic scene from Claremont widely across the state. Two days later, Governor Clinton—as a "new Democrat," a supporter of the death penalty—allowed Arkansas to execute a mentally incompetent killer. His staff, meanwhile, had accepted an offer for the Clintons to appear on *Sixty Minutes,* the widely watched CBS news program, to be broadcast this time immediately after the Super Bowl.

The Clinton segment was taped in Boston and edited later by CBS, with the beleaguered candidate developing much the same general line he had put forward at the Sperling breakfast in September. Hillary Clinton added heroically that she was not "some little woman standing by my man like Tammy Wynette.† I'm sitting here because I love him and I respect him and I honor what he's been through and what we've been through together."

It's probable that the dual *Sixty Minutes* interview—one of the most dramatic moments in any political year—saved Clinton's campaign, in New Hampshire and nationally. His statewide polls showed that, while his rise to a lead over Tsongas had slowed to a stop, he had suffered no sharp loss of support. Nor did he do so when, on the day after *Sixty Minutes,* Gennifer Flowers

---

*Years later, when he was president, Clinton finally acknowledged in an affidavit for independent counsel Kenneth Starr that he had had an affair with Flowers years earlier. No details were given, nor was her 1992 account in the *Star* verified.

†A country-music star, well known at that time for her recording of a song called *Stand By Your Man.*

herself appeared in New York at a *Star*-sponsored news conference, claiming defiantly to have had a twelve-year love affair with Clinton. She also played some of her tapes—but only selected excerpts, which did not quite confirm her story and added nothing to her credibility.

Then, on February 6, less than twelve days before the primary, Clinton—now beginning to look like a political punchboard—suffered another damaging charge, this time in the respectable and respected *Wall Street Journal*. In its news columns, the *Journal* reported that a retired colonel, Eugene Holmes, formerly an army recruiter, said that in 1969 Clinton had signed up for the ROTC at the University of Arkansas, which enabled him to receive a draft deferment and stay out of service in the Vietnam War. This, too, was an old story that in his gubernatorial campaigns Clinton had refuted by pointing out that he had given up the deferment and been reclassified 1-A on October 30, 1969—but then had drawn such a high number in the December 1 draft lottery that he was never called for induction. Colonel Holmes had previously supported this version of events.

That weekend Clinton went back to Arkansas to recover from a brief illness, and suddenly the bottom fell out of his New Hampshire campaign, his poll number falling like a stone from 37 to 17, and Paul Tsongas—the Massachusetts neighbor who had been campaigning in New Hampshire for nearly a year—surging just as suddenly into a substantial lead. Returning quickly, the Clinton party had only just set foot on the ground in New Hampshire when they were staggered yet again.

An aide, George Stephanopoulos, was handed a copy of a letter written to Colonel Holmes from Oxford, England, where in 1969 the twenty-three-year-old Bill Clinton had been studying on a Rhodes Scholarship. In the long letter, Clinton thanked Holmes for "saving me from the draft," told of his deep opposition at the time to the Vietnam War, against which he had demonstrated in the United States and in England, and expressed the hope that his letter would help Holmes understand "how so many fine young people . . . find themselves still loving their country but loathing the military."

Crucially, however, the twenty-two-year-old letter also explained why Clinton had not, after all, joined the Arkansas ROTC but had instead made himself draft-eligible again "to maintain my political viability within the system." This tended to prove *his* version of the draft story—that he had voluntarily made himself available for induction rather than accept the safety of an ROTC deferment.

Once again a national television appearance may well have rescued Clinton. A day after the Oxford letter surfaced, Clinton appeared on ABC's *Nightline,* with Ted Koppel, who read the letter in full. Clinton termed it "a true reflection" of his conflicted feelings in 1969—which many in his generation had shared—and insisted that the letter confirmed what he had been saying for years about his draft record. His performance was strong, effective—even aggressive. But polls did not reflect any significant gain in New Hampshire.

When the Democratic primary returns came in on February 18, Paul Tsongas was the easy winner. But he defeated Clinton by a smaller margin than the self-labeled "Comeback Kid" had amassed over the rest of the field in what was, if not a victory, still the most important political development in New Hampshire that winter—or maybe anywhere in the nation in 1992.

New Hampshire put an effective end to primary campaigning in either party—though Buchanan constituted a major problem of diverted resources for the president, while landing stinging blows here and there on the economic issue, and Clinton and Jerry Brown had a particularly contentious showdown in New York. By the time the national conventions met in the summer of 1992—the Democrats in New York, the Republicans in Houston, the president's adopted hometown—George Bush and Bill Clinton were confirmed as the Republican and Democratic presidential nominees.

Displaying loyalty as usual, Bush ignored poll data and some Republican opposition, and again named Dan Quayle as his running mate. Clinton, spurning conventional notions of geographical balance, made the unusual choice of another young southerner, Senator Al Gore of Tennessee, just across the river from Arkansas. The Clinton-Gore combination—of youth, good looks, two "new Democrats," two stylish young wives— soon proved more important than old-fashioned geographical "balance."

At one point the stage seemed set for a traditional presidential campaign. The Republican nominees had triumphed in five of the last six such elections, and had held the White House in twenty of the previous twenty-four years, including the last twelve. But 1992 soon looked as if it might be different: For one thing, a combination of George Bush's difficulties (economic recession, Buchanan's damaging insurgency, sluggish campaigning) and Bill Clinton's strengths (a new face, a "new Democrat," a national sense that it was truly "time for a change," spirited campaigning) made the so-called Republican "lock" seem less secure. The Democratic nominees therefore entered the general election campaign not only with an early lead in the polls (so had Dukakis) but with better prospects for ultimate victory than the party had known since Lyndon Johnson demolished Barry Goldwater in 1964.

More important was the likelihood, appearing on February 20, just two days after the New Hampshire primary, of still another candidate, independent of the two established parties: the fabulously rich Texas businessman Ross Perot. Third-party and independent candidates were not unusual in U.S. politics; the most famous example probably was that of ex-president Theodore Roosevelt, running on the Progressive (Bull Moose) ticket in 1912, helping to defeat a Republican president, William Howard Taft, and probably ensuring the election of the Democratic candidate, Woodrow Wilson. More recently the third-party candidacy of Governor George Wallace of Alabama had contributed to the razor-thin victory of Richard Nixon over Hubert Humphrey in 1968; but neither Wallace nor the independent John Anderson, running in 1980, and not even TR, ever had come close to winning outright. For a time in early 1992, poll figures and an uprising of voters fed up with "politics as usual," made it seem possible that Ross Perot might actually become president of the United States.*

The Perot candidacy resulted from the determined efforts of voters impatient with the two-party system and ready to turn to

*For instance, in late April, a *Washington Post*/ABC News poll showed respondents favoring Bush by 36 percent to 31 for Clinton and 30 for Perot. One later poll actually had Perot leading both party candidates by a narrow margin.

a more promising alternative—as Perot said, and they thought, he was—and from effective television appearances by the Texas billionaire. He turned out to have a gift for making complex matters seem simple, and his extraordinary business success (in computer services) lent him much credibility. Perot pursued no special issue—such as Wallace's appeal to segregationists in 1968—but was attractive to all kinds of voters, Democrats, independents, and Republicans alike, who felt they were not being well served, or even listened to, by the established parties and their candidates.

The crucial event that melded Perot and the public discontent was the Texan's appearance on a television program with Larry King of CNN, on February 20. As the interview opened, Perot denied that he would be a candidate, as was already widely rumored; but by the end of the show he had advised King's viewers that if they actually wanted Ross Perot to run for president, they should get to work and put his name on the ballot in fifty states.* If they did, he said, he'd pay for his own campaign, and his volunteers would have to contribute only five dollars apiece.

The response was overwhelming and the Perot "draft," thus stimulated by the man himself, moved ahead with what George Bush once had called "Big Mo"—so much so that the supposedly volunteer campaign took on several professionals (including the same Ed Rollins who had advised House Republican candidates to distance themselves from President Bush in 1990, and Hamilton Jordan, the former chief of staff and strategist for President

---

*A task made easier by the efforts of John Anderson as an independent candidate twelve years earlier, in 1980.

Ross Perot thus got out of the campaign himself, despite the call he had so ringingly issued on *Larry King Live* back in February, imploring his followers to "stay in the ring" and fight for their beliefs, even after he was elected. Perot did not even bother, in his withdrawal announcement, to thank the volunteers he had abandoned.

CHAPTER NINE

GEORGE BUSH HAD strong reasons to believe, as he began the autumn election campaign in 1992, that foreign policy was an asset that would carry him through. Not only was he the experienced and steady leader who had organized and won Desert Storm; Americans had relied on his party for years as the best choice to defend the nation and advance its interests abroad. And the record was impressive.

The Cold War had been won. Eastern Europe was independent. The Soviet Union was history; so were the Sandinistas in Nicaragua and Noriega in Panama. Germany was united, and no one was much worried anymore, or needed to be, about the threat of nuclear extinction. Bush personally had reached arms-reduction agreements, first with Gorbachev in 1991, then with Boris Yeltsin in the new Russia in 1992. He also had supported sanctions that helped bring an end to the apartheid government of South Africa, and had promoted active peace negotiations between Arabs and Jews.

The very success of the United States in the Cold War, however, and the absence or diminution of other threats meant that foreign policy was no longer the overwhelming national priority it had been. Nor was the Republican Party any longer able to convince Americans that it was needed in power to defend the nation's security (from what? some commentators asked). A lengthy recession and high unemployment in the United States had shifted voters' worries from foreign threats to the "pocketbook issues"—upon which the Democratic Party had been focused since the New Deal.

With Ross Perot off the board, moreover, active anti-Bush sentiment, which had been divided between Perot and Clinton supporters, suddenly was concentrated behind Bill Clinton—an effect not foreseen by the Bush campaign. So when the Democratic nominee and his running mate departed New York in July after their national convention, embarking on a long-planned bus trip through some prime target states,* Clinton and Gore led Bush and Quayle by 55 to 31. Of course, it was generally supposed, the Republican coronation of Bush at the national convention in Houston later in the summer would close the gap.

It didn't—not quite, and for several reasons. Well before the convention, for one thing, though Dan Quayle was the president's certain vice presidential choice, concern continued to be felt by the campaign staff that Quayle would be a "drag" on the ticket; voters in both parties told poll takers they were not happy that Quayle should be a "heartbeat" away from the White House.

Bush's campaign team also was dissatisfied with White House staff cooperation, and was urging him to bring back Jim

---

*The old-line industrial states from New York and New Jersey through Pennsylvania, Ohio, and Illinois. Michigan was another target state, as was Missouri. The Clinton-Gore bus tour wound up in St. Louis.

Baker as his chief of staff and, in effect, campaign manager. Baker, however, made clear his desire to remain as secretary of state and out of domestic politics.

Another question for Republicans that summer: Would the strong antiabortion plank written into their platforms for 1984 and 1988 be retained for 1992? There was little reason to doubt that it would be, considering the power of right-wing forces among Republican delegates at Houston. But once again, the problem was the right wing's basic, unforgotten and only slightly concealed mistrust of George Bush, the New Englander turned Texan, the eastern moderate converted—maybe—to southwestern conservatism.

As a presidential aspirant in 1980, Bush had taken a pro-choice position on the Supreme Court's *Roe v. Wade* decision. Only after he was chosen as Ronald Reagan's running mate did his attitude harden. It had continued to harden during his vice presidential years and his first term in the White House, to the point that by 1992 he supported the "gag rule" preventing workers in federally funded clinics from even discussing abortion with pregnant women. Still, one about-face might presage another, in the nervous view of religious conservatives like Pat Robertson, Jerry Falwell, and not a few others.

Even before the platform committee began its deliberations, therefore, Bush tried to remove any remaining doubt. He announced that he would do "what I think is right" and back the antiabortion plank at whatever political cost. But on the same day that the platform committee approved the plank, 84 to 16, Bush seemed to retreat. Asked in a TV interview what he'd do if one of his granddaughters wanted an abortion, he said he'd "encourage her not to do that. . . . But of course, I'd stand by my child [*sic*]." Which, he was reminded, could mean only that the final decision would be hers.

"Whose else could it be?" Bush asked, as if that were self-evident.

He seemed not to realize that he was stating the pro-choice position—to have an abortion, or not, was the woman's decision to make—or that what he would do about the situation of someone in his own family differed sharply from what he and his party insisted in their platform was proper and moral for other American women.

The platform committee went serenely on to oppose any legislation recognizing same-sex marriages and to proclaim that some in the media, the entertainment industry, academics and the Democratic party were waging a "guerrilla war" against American values. In a year when nine million Americans were unemployed and the nation was preoccupied with a sluggish economy, the platform's emphasis on such "social issues" was setting a different, nearly irrelevant tone for a convention the nation was watching on television.

The platform makers might have taken their cue from a speech by Bush himself in which he had proclaimed that "the president should try to set a moral tone for this nation"—an obvious dig at Bill Clinton as a "womanizer" and draft dodger. In fact, Bush said, a "central issue" of the election should be: "Who do you trust to renew America's moral purpose?" Not, conspicuously, who can best help you put bread on the table and send the kids to college?

The convention program, as it unfolded, seemed in many ways to confirm the emphasis on "morality" and to point to "family values," not the economy, as the real issue. National Chairman

Rich Bond fiercely attacked Hillary Clinton for, he said, comparing "marriage and the family to slavery."* Bond and Quayle, in separate speeches, scalded the news media for supposedly favoring Clinton over Bush—the old Republican complaint about the "liberal press."† In an accusatory speech, Quayle's wife, Marilyn, reminded the convention that not everyone in the baby-boom generation (hers and Clinton's) "demonstrated, dropped out, took drugs, joined in the sexual revolution or dodged the draft." That pejoratively linked all those activities as Democratic choices, and took another cut at Clinton.

Marilyn Quayle's husband, the scourge of television's *Murphy Brown* and of unwed mothers generally, bore down on the family values theme: "For me, family comes first." And it was wrong and untrue to claim "that every so-called lifestyle alternative is morally equivalent." Then Quayle hit the "morality" theme with a claim not often heard at a *political* convention when, theoretically, a party seeks to broaden its appeal beyond its own membership: "The gap between us and our opponents is a cultural divide. . . . not just a difference between conservative and liberal. It is a difference between fighting for what is right and refusing to see what is wrong."

Not in more than a quarter century had Americans been told so clearly that political differences were *moral* differences. Many listening to Quayle in 1992 heard echoes of Barry Goldwater outlining conservative beliefs in 1964, then declaring: "Anyone who joins us in all sincerity, we welcome. Those who do not care

*A considerable stretch on what Ms. Clinton had written in a magazine article nearly 20 years earlier.

†As recently as 1948, however, President Truman had been reelected while castigating what he called the "Republican press."

for our cause, we don't expect to enter our ranks in any case." But Quayle offered no hint of Goldwater's more conciliatory conclusion ("We must not see malice in honest differences of opinion").

Worse—at least in the eyes of some more traditional Republicans, the kind Prescott Bush had been and George H. W. Bush once was considered—was a thunderous opening-night speech by Pat Buchanan, the president's "mean and ugly" antagonist from New Hampshire. Buchanan delivered a good soldier's endorsement for Bush, as had been required by campaign officials, described the just-concluded Democratic convention witheringly as "the greatest single exhibition of cross-dressing in American political history," and took the obligatory crack at Clinton for "dodg[ing] the draft." But the red meat of his speech was in two fire-breathing passages.

One was his description of what he said Clinton as president would impose on the nation—"abortion on demand, a litmus test for the Supreme Court, homosexual rights, discrimination against religious schools, women in combat . . . not the kind of change we can tolerate in a nation that we still call God's country."

The other was Buchanan's rancorous definition of what "this election is about."

It is about who we are. It is about what we believe. It is about what we stand for as Americans. There is a religious war going on in our country for the soul of America. It is a cultural war, as critical to the kind of nation we will one day be as the Cold War itself. And in that struggle for the soul of America, Clinton [and] Clinton are on the other side, and George Bush is on our side.[1]

Watching on the home screen,* I was amazed that the Republicans were allowing such abrasive and divisive messages—"religious war," "cultural divide"—to go out as official expressions of their party in national convention in 1992. And how could George Bush—the president but a candidate for reelection running behind in all the polls—have allowed such spokesmen (especially Pat Buchanan, who was essentially an also-ran) to take over and exploit what would be the party's most important moment of exposure in the national spotlight? That moment could and should have been used to extol the nation's future under the economic program Bush was supposed to be including in his forthcoming acceptance of the presidential nomination.

Later Germond and Witcover reported in *Mad as Hell* that the president's ranking political operatives had read Buchanan's warlike text in advance and, incredibly enough, had seen nothing in it but what they wanted to see—his endorsement of Bush.[2] Even more significantly, as the Quayles and Bond and Buchanan burned Republican bridges behind them, the campaign strategists *still* did not understand that such nationally televised convention oratory was alienating the half—or perhaps more—of the populace that did not feel itself or its neighbors to be in a "religious" or a "cultural" war, might even be pro-choice, and did not quite see George Bush as a warrior struggling for the nation's soul. They wanted him, or someone, to fight for the nation's pocketbook.

The assiduous Germond and Witcover suggest a plausible reason for what seemed to be the obtuse Republican manage-

*The national party conventions of 1992 were the first since 1964 that I had not covered as a reporter.

ment of a convention—really a TV spectacle—that could make or break the struggling Bush candidacy. Jim Lake, the campaign communications director, told them: "I had no idea [the tone of the convention] would cause as much backlash as it did. We still felt we had to, we still did have to, tie down the base. We hadn't done that yet and that was why we wanted Buchanan here."

To which the Democratic strategist James Carville replied sarcastically: "If you use your convention to get your base back, that's not a very good way to use a convention. You've just got to take your base for granted."[3]

Not everyone would agree with the second sentence of Carville's remark. In this particular case, however, it would have made much more sense for Bush and his campaign staff to "tie down" the party's conservative base *before* the convention (if they could). They surely should have realized, moreover, that the right-wing delegates who cheered Pat Buchanan and Dan Quayle in Houston were by no means representative of the whole voting population or even of all conservatives, let alone the television audience and the Republican Party. Not to mention that the nation palpably was more concerned with the economy than with supposed religious and cultural wars.

To top off a strange convention week, Bush in his acceptance speech did not, after all, give the nation much of an idea of what he had in mind for the economy. In the glimpses he did offer were several tax cuts—but no more "read my lips" pledges—including the shopworn proposal to reduce the capital gains tax, and a scheme to allow taxpayers to earmark 10 percent of their payments for deficit reduction. Even this meager fare was not to be proposed to Congress until after the election in November, which made the promises problematic at best.

Nevertheless, and despite the considerable national reaction against those sulfurous convention speeches, Bush registered a substantial gain in the polls—though nowhere near what he needed. A *Washington Post*/ABC News survey immediately after Houston found Clinton leading by only 49 to 40, a substantial drop from his strong earlier leads—but not exactly the "closing of the gap" that had been expected. Without Buchanan's brimstone, and if the president had put forward an attractive economic proposal, who knows what the polls might have registered?

From the moment Ross Perot pulled out of the campaign, on the last day of the Democratic National Convention, the foremost question on the minds of journalists and political professionals in both parties was whether the Texas billionaire would return to it. Some thought the real question was *when;* a few even asked *how.* No one doubted that Perot's abrupt, poorly explained withdrawal had damaged his personal credibility and interrupted the momentum of the volunteer movement that had looked so promising in the spring.

Some of Perot's most dedicated supporters, with his approval, gathered in Dallas on July 18, two days after his startling withdrawal. Their deliberations produced mostly an abortive "draft" movement; those who knew Perot best, however, insisted he would not be pushed into anything he didn't want to do. And indeed, Perot stubbornly refused to accede. The meetings did encourage some of his supporters, some of the general public, and probably even Perot himself to think that, eventually, he could reenter the campaign—as he himself suggested, pulling an "October surprise."

In the early weeks of the campaign, Perot, as he also suggested, was an "800-pound gorilla"; nobody knew what he would do, but probably no one could stop him from doing it. Another, calmer group of supporters, meeting at the end of July, knew better than to pursue the draft idea; instead they decided to continue the campaign to get Perot on the ballot in fifty states—exerting unsubtle pressure on him to meet the test he himself had set back in the winter, in the original Larry King broadcast.

Perot agreed to finance the ballot campaigns, again boosting the idea that he would eventually reenter the race. He continued, rather as if he were an addict, to make the TV talk-show rounds, and published a paperback book at last detailing his deficit reduction plan—conventional but harsh spending cuts and tax increases. He also advocated a gasoline tax that could rise to fifty cents a gallon, an idea first put forward by John Anderson in his Republican, later independent, candidacy in 1980—and that had brought Anderson only a third-place finish, far behind Reagan and Carter.

Perot continued to maintain, not persuasively, that the decision whether to run again would be made by his volunteers—although he knew from the postwithdrawal meetings that of course they wanted his reentry. On September 19, ballot position in fifty states had been attained—Arizona was the last. Meanwhile, however, Perot's poll numbers had not returned to the heights attained before his pullout. He nevertheless invited both parties to send missions to meet with him in Dallas, ostensibly to convince him that they would "step up to the plate" on the economy and other issues.

On September 28, 1992, therefore, both parties put themselves in the demeaning position of trying, in reality, to talk Perot out of running—although, to a number of political observers, he seemed to pose more of a threat to Bush than to Clinton. When the Democratic group met Perot, he again tried the familiar my-volunteers-will-decide ploy. Vernon Jordan, a close friend of Clinton's, replied with some impatience: "Now, Ross, you know *you'll* make that decision, not your volunteers."[4]

By then, having a wide poll lead of which all sides were aware, Clinton held the stronger hand,* not only with Perot but in continuing negotiations with the Bush strategists on the timing and format of the televised debates that had become a fixture in American presidential campaigns. Bush wanted four, each with a panel of inquiring reporters, as in 1988; Clinton preferred a single moderator and, wary of sensational last-minute charges he would not have time to refute, set a nonnegotiable deadline: no debates after October 19, two weeks before election day.

Both sides, however, needed and wanted to debate: Clinton to prove his readiness for the presidency, Bush to pick up speed in the polls and emphasize the choice—as he frequently tried to frame it—between his experienced leadership and the untried Clinton's youth and unproved reliability. With Clinton so far ahead, however, and with Bush taking repeated hits for his alleged unwillingness to debate, the outcome was nearly inevitable. The two sides settled for ninety-minute debates on October 11, 15, and 19 (Clinton's deadline), with the October 15 session to be in a "town-meeting format"—proposed by Clinton himself, with the Republicans unexpectedly agreeing. The first and last debates would have a panel of questioners.

*The Democrats also had "locked up" the major states of California and New York and held commanding leads in a number of others.

Perot was to be included, having surprised no one by reentering the campaign on October 1, in a news conference in which he typically engaged in a shouting match with reporters. By then, however, no one but his most fanatic supporters was taking him seriously as a likely president.

In the first debate* in St. Louis, Bush continued a campaign tactic he had been using regularly—criticizing Clinton for having taken part in antiwar demonstrations while a student at Oxford during the Vietnam War. Demonstrating against "your own country . . . on foreign soil," the president insisted, was "wrong." Whereupon Clinton, who had heard the charge before, and was expecting it again, compared Bush's tactic to the smears of Joe McCarthy in the fifties, and pointed out that Senator Prescott Bush then had opposed McCarthyism. Now his son was "wrong to attack my patriotism," Clinton told the president. "I was opposed to the war but I love my country."

In Richmond, four nights later, with Carole Simpson of ABC News presiding over the "town meeting," two early questioners from the floor implored the candidates to stop trashing their opponents and pursuing "the wants of your spin doctorism and your political parties."

Perot agreed immediately: "Let's get off the personalities, and let's talk about . . . the things that concern the American people."

Bush, however, stuck to his practiced line: "My argument

*Quotations from the 1992 campaign debates are taken from www.debates.org/pages/debhis92.html and other published accounts.

with Governor Clinton—you can call it mud wrestling, but I think it's fair to put it in focus—is I am deeply troubled by someone who demonstrates in a foreign land when his country's at war . . . that's what I feel passionately about."

Earlier in a rambling answer, Bush had cited the fact that he had joined the Navy at age eighteen in World War II—thus managing to remind the audience of Clinton's failure to serve in the Vietnam War. Clinton, however, refused to rise to even this bait; he told the first questioner that he agreed with her and therefore would not take time to reply to Bush's comments.

He also agreed with the second questioner, and Perot the phrase maker immediately said that he'd "take the pledge" against negative attacks. Bush then agreed—but in a hesitant manner. The presidency involved a lot of things that were not specific issues, he said, citing "caring" and "strength," but added: "[I]n principle, though, I'll take your point."

If that was a pledge, it was good for only four days. In the third debate, at Michigan State University, Bush returned to another familiar campaign theme: "[T]his pattern that has plagued [Clinton] . . . about trying to have it both ways on all these issues." Later he cited "this question about trust . . . a pattern by Governor Clinton of saying one thing to please one group" but something else to other groups. This, Bush insisted, was a "dangerous pattern," particularly if replicated in the Oval Office.

Clinton had reminded the Michigan State audience of the Richmond town meeting, when questioners "told us they wanted us to stop talking about each other and start talking about Americans and their problems." Now he seemed to have had enough:

I really can't believe Mister Bush is still trying to make trust an issue after "read my lips" and [his pledge to provide] 15 million new jobs and embracing what he called voodoo economics and embracing an export enhancement program for farms he threatened to veto, and going all around the country giving out money in programs he once opposed.

As polls and commentary later confirmed, Clinton had the better of these exchanges—though he, too, at Michigan State, had been goaded finally to abandon the "no personalities" pledge he and Perot (and Bush grudgingly) had taken at Richmond. But the most significant moment in the debates had been in the Richmond town meeting after a questioner asked all the candidates to say how the national debt (she obviously meant the recession) had "personally affected each of your lives. And if it hasn't, how can you honestly find a cure for the economic problems of the common people?"

Perhaps puzzled by the questioner's reference to the "national debt," the president said first, "Obviously it has a lot to do with interest rates. . . . I want to think [my grandchildren] are going to be able to afford an education. . . . Maybe I—get it wrong. Are you suggesting that if somebody has means that the national debt doesn't affect them?" Looking puzzled, he added: "I'm not sure I get it. Help me with the question and I'll try to answer it."

It was a remarkable and embarrassing moment—the president of the United States asking for help on a citizen's question he clearly didn't understand. The questioner, still referring to the "national debt," explained that she wanted to know "how has it affected you? And if you have no experience in it, how can you help us if you don't know what we're feeling."

Moderator Simpson explained that the questioner really meant "the recession."

"Well," Bush said, brightening, "you ought to be in the White House for a day and hear what I hear and see what I see and read the mail and touch the people that I touch from time to time." At a black church, he went on, he had recently "read in the bulletin about teen-age pregnancies, about the difficulties that families are having to make ends meet. . . . I mean, you've got to care. Everybody cares if people aren't doing very well."

He could not seem to stop. "But I don't think it's fair to say, 'You haven't had cancer, therefore you don't know what it's like.' . . . [I]n terms of the recession, of course you feel it when you're president of the United States." When at last he finished, he told the questioner, "I'm glad to clarify it."

Backstage Clinton's staff already was celebrating, even before Clinton himself answered. They knew the president had stumbled badly, first by his incomprehension—should a president ever appear muddled?—then by talking about his grandchildren's education, claiming to have read about poverty in a church bulletin, citing the White House mail as his source of information, "touch[ing] the people that I touch"—but only *from time to time*" (italics added).

Clinton ambled across the stage toward the questioner, asked her to tell him again how "it's affected you. . . . You know people who've lost their jobs and lost their homes?" On the TV screen, at least, he seemed to be talking directly to her. After her brief reply, he said, "I'll tell you how it's affected me."

As the governor of a small state, he'd seen "middle class

people, their taxes have gone up in Washington and their services have gone down, while the wealthy have gotten tax cuts." In his state, when people lost jobs "there's a good chance I'll know them by their names." If factories closed and businesses went bankrupt, "I know them." And all through the thirteen months he had been campaigning, he had met and talked to "people that have lost their jobs, lost their livelihood, lost their health insurance. . . . It is because we've had 12 years of trickle-down economics. We've gone from first to twelfth in the world in wages. We've had four years where we've produced no private sector jobs. Most people are working harder for less money than they were making 10 years ago."

A television camera picked up President Bush stealing a glance at his watch, as if bored with the discussion.*

Clinton, not knowing this, proceeded with his response: ". . . just people saying I'm going to fix it, but what are we going to do? What I think we have to do is invest in American jobs, American education, control American health care costs and bring the American people together again."

Whatever else the debates had accomplished, they had not restored George H. W. Bush to the lead expected of an incumbent who once had registered a 91 percent approval rating. Polls showed the Democratic nominee, Bill Clinton, with a wide popular-vote lead; and careful calculations in both camps suggested that he would win with more than three hundred electoral votes. Two

*After the debate, aides explained Bush thought his opponents were talking beyond the time limit agreed upon in the debate negotiations. Even so, the television shot was damaging.

weeks before Election Day, Bush faced the rare prospect of being voted out of office after only one term, the fate of only three other elected presidents*—William Howard Taft, Herbert Hoover, and Jimmy Carter—in the twentieth century.

Bush can never be accused of having given up—as, indeed, no incumbent ever should give up, considering all the advantages a sitting president should have over even an opponent as adept as Bill Clinton had proved to be. For the remaining two weeks of the campaign, after the third debate, the president drove himself relentlessly about the country, pounding away primarily at Clinton's long-ago role in anti-Vietnam demonstrations abroad, and what Bush called his "waffling" at home—saying one thing here, another there. These indicated a slippery character not to be trusted, Bush reiterated, and personal "trust" became the theme of the president's campaign.

"Who do you trust," Bush frequently shouted, "to be president of the United States?" The words sometimes changed—the basic question never did.

For his part Clinton remained determinedly "on message"—about the economic recession and the hard times people were having. He used Bush's stumbling responses at the Richmond town meeting to suggest that the president "just didn't get it"—he didn't understand the consequences of his economic policies. Clinton was not hesitant, either, to remind voters of the cut-and-slash Bush campaign against Dukakis only four years earlier ("Don't forget that Mr. Bush has said himself that he'd do any-

*Lyndon Johnson withdrew from the race in 1968 and was not actually defeated as an incumbent.

thing to get reelected"), suggesting that Bush's "trust" charges were of the same negative stamp.

Three major incidents marked those final, postdebate weeks:

In keeping with Bush's emphasis on Clinton's more than twenty-years-past behavior during the Vietnam War, Republicans had cast sinister implications on a tourist trip Clinton made from England to Moscow in 1969—one of sixty thousand Americans who visited the Soviet Union that year. *Newsweek* then reported that several pages appeared to be missing from Clinton's passport file in the State Department, and Bush himself questioned the Moscow trip on *Larry King Live** on October 7. But when elements in the press suggested a new "Dukakis strategy," the president dropped the matter.

Later, however, as the Bush campaign was making a desperate finish run, the State Department was forced to disclose that the assistant secretary for consular affairs, Elizabeth M. Tamposi, a Republican on John Sununu's patronage, had ordered a search of Clinton's passport file, stored in a warehouse in Suitland, Maryland. At first, the search was said to be in response to Freedom of Information requests; then the State Department admitted that it was "clearly a mistake" and fingered Tamposi as the culprit.†

---

*The frequency with which King appears in any narrative of the 1992 election suggests how important "talk" radio and TV had become to political campaigners.

†After the election, Bush fired Tamposi, who said she'd acted on indirect orders from the White House through another assistant secretary, Steven K. Berry. The search had been requested by an aide to James A. Baker III, Berry had told her. Several investigations resulted. Baker conceded he'd known of the search while it was going on, but responsibility never was fixed on him. Berry wound up working for Congress.

The matter became a political plus for Bill Clinton, particularly when it was disclosed that his mother's file had also been searched (as was Ross Perot's). Clinton treated the whole matter as something of a sad joke, a frantic last gasp by a frustrated opponent—"political hacks rifling through my mother's files trying to find dirt." Sarcastically, he referred to his mother as "a well-known subversive" and added: "It would be funny if it weren't so pathetic."

On October 25, on *Sixty Minutes,* Ross Perot returned to the headlines with a spectacular explanation of his withdrawal from the campaign in July. Conceding that he had no proof, he said he'd been warned that the Bush campaign was threatening to disrupt his daughter's wedding in August. "I could not allow my daughter's happiest day of her life [*sic*] . . . to be ruined . . . it was a risk I could not take." So he had taken himself out of the campaign.

The White House immediately denied this as "just crazy," and Perot never did claim or produce anything that could be considered proof. Instead speculation increased that when he had dropped out in July, he had been planning to reenter in October after bypassing most of the drudgery he would have undergone and the press scrutiny he would have received had he campaigned throughout August and September. Perot wound up in an expensive blaze of paid television, pushing his deficit reduction scheme in a bare-bones format featuring himself, a variety of charts, and a pointer. His productions drew large audiences but produced no significant increase in his third-place poll standing.

Bush's supporters claimed that he was "surging" in the final days of the campaign, a possibility steadfastly denied, in a war of poll takers, by Stan Greenberg, Clinton's official number cruncher. But on Friday, October 30, just before the voting on Tuesday, the Bush "surge," even if it was happening, was severely jolted. That day (as briefly noted in chapter 4), former Reagan defense secretary Caspar Weinberger was indicted for having misled Congress in 1987; Weinberger was charged with having falsely testified that he had taken no notes of certain meetings in 1986 and 1987, when it was alleged that he had.

Among documents released with the indictment was a Weinberger note about a meeting of the National Security Council on January 7, 1986, when President Reagan "decided to go with Israeli-Iranian offer to release our five hostages in return for sale of 4,000 [missiles]."

Weinberger listed himself and Secretary of State George Shultz as opposed to the scheme, but included "VP"—unmistakably a reference to George Bush—among those who "favored" it. But Bush had steadfastly insisted that he knew nothing of an arms-for-hostages deal until he learned the truth from a Senate Intelligence Committee briefing in December 1986. The Weinberger note suggested that he had known about the proposed swap at least a year earlier.

Clinton quickly turned the "trust" issue back on Bush. The Weinberger note, he said, "not only contradicts the president's claims but also diminishes the credibility of the presidency." But Bush, again on Larry King's show, denied that the note was new evidence and again said that he and Reagan had regarded the Iran matter not as an arms-for-hostage swap but rather as an effort to create a diplomatic opening to Iran. That did not square—as numerous callers-in to the King show made clear—with the direct assertion in Weinberger's note that "VP" favored a swap of four thousand missiles for five hostages. For once, talk-show campaigning had backfired.

Many Bush supporters believed, and some still may, (a) that Bush was "surging" toward a comeback victory before the Weinberger indictment, and (b) that its announcement on the Friday before the Tuesday election day was a campaign maneuver by liberal Democrats working in the office of independent counsel Lawrence E. Walsh. Neither charge ever has been proven and both are substantially contradicted—(a) by Stan Greenberg's repeated assurances to the Clinton campaign staff, and also by the fact that the supposed Bush "surge" was predicated on a "trend" that might or might not have continued, with or without the indictment; and (b) by the fact that Walsh was a Republican. If he had wanted to delay the announcement of the Weinberger indictment, it's hard to believe he couldn't have done it; and if he had found himself thwarted in that aim by "liberal Democrats" on his staff, surely he could have said so. He never did.

It seems likely nevertheless that Perot's bizarre explanation of his withdrawal damaged him, that the passport fiasco damaged Bush, and that the Weinberger note at least threw the "trust" charge back in Bush's face—so that, in the end, these events clinched for Bill Clinton an election that he probably would have won anyway. Actual results, which were not really close, tend to bear out that conclusion.

On election night in 1992, after 55.24 percent of eligible voters (against only 50.1 percent in 1988) had cast their ballots, Clinton won 43 percent of the popular vote and carried 370 electoral votes from 32 states and the District of Columbia. The incumbent president, George H. W. Bush, won 38 percent of the vote and 168 electoral votes in eighteen states. Ross Perot got 19 percent of the popular votes and carried not a single state; it's hard to believe, after the spectacular beginnings of his candidacy, that he had not squandered a real opportunity with his personal idiosyncrasies and his reluctance to get wholeheartedly "into the arena."

It's often suggested, nevertheless, that Bush would have won if Perot had not been in the race—his 38 plus Perot's 19 percent of the popular vote equals 57. That assumes what can't be assumed—that all of Perot's popular vote would have gone to Bush and none to Clinton. Perot's candidacy, after all, grew out of public dissatisfaction with the existing political system and what was seen as an ineffective government. Bush represented both, so that it's unlikely he could have taken even 12 percent of those who voted for Perot, to give himself a bare-bones 50 percent of the popular vote—against 50 percent for Clinton, who in that case theoretically would have had the other 7 percent of Perot's vote.

Or, if Perot's popular vote is split down the middle, the result is Clinton, about 51 percent; Bush, 46. Since Perot carried no states, moreover, even if most of his popular support had gone to Bush, the president probably could not have put together a victory in the electoral college. In short, Bush was soundly defeated in a three-man race—and almost certainly would have been in a one-on-one showdown with Bill Clinton.

CHAPTER TEN

On election night when Bush had conceded to Clinton, and the White House in its weary sadness had dimmed and paused for a few hours, one could loiter on Pennsylvania Avenue and marvel anew at the magic in this old system of ours. No tanks guarded the White House gates. No troops cordoned the streets. The greatest political power on the face of the earth had been taken from one man and given to another, and it was done with only the riffle of an autumn breeze around the big house that George Washington built.

—Hugh Sidey in *Time*, November 16, 1992

ONE OF THE INSISTENT NOTIONS of American politics is that George Herbert Walker Bush, the forty-first president of the United States, was a nice man—whether, in his time, you were for him or against him. Few beliefs are more heavily attested, by adversaries as well as friends; most of Bush's career, as well as his present life, supports the description. Those of us who were active during his White House tenure (1989–93) as well as that of his son, George W. Bush, (2002–?) have been able to see for ourselves the plain fact that the father was then a more relaxed, approachable, and less driven, perhaps single-minded, man than his son is now. With which, for instance, would one rather spend a social evening?

I well remember a good friend, not to my knowledge pronouncedly liberal or conservative, who on the strength of his books was invited to spend a weekend at Camp David with the first President Bush. He came back singing Bush's praises—not for any attitude the president had expressed on a subject of world or national import but because George Bush was such a genial opponent in pitching horseshoes and such a pleasant host for a convivial weekend. Not at all like a president!

I did not doubt my friend's impression. George H. W. Bush *is* a nice man in the general sense that he has a sunny disposition, a sense of humor, great loyalty to his friends, and dedication to the public service, and is always polite and circumspect in his dealings with others. His manners are impeccable. A good host indeed. That endless outflow of thank-you notes, some written before *Air Force 2* or, later, *Air Force 1* was off the ground, may have been driven by ambition for the future—but it was not the product of a selfish or a self-absorbed man who failed to appreciate those who helped him along the way.

Yet this very reputation for good personal relations has helped to camouflage—not to conceal from anyone who looks closely—the overweening ambition that, as has so often been the case with "nice" men, was the flaw of George H. W. Bush, politician. He said candidly that he would "do anything to get elected"—and proved it twice in 1988, first with the attack ad that skewered Bob Dole in the New Hampshire primary; then in the general election campaign with his relentless assault on Michael Dukakis as a man unfit to be president.

His efforts in 1992 to cast doubt on Bill Clinton's patriotism, most of them based on the activities of a young man twenty years earlier, were less glaring but just as real. To this evidence could be added the effortless adoption, in Texas in 1964, of Barry Goldwater's politics and the unfilial suppression, that year, of Prescott Bush's different views. Changing circumstances were followed by the expedient switch to quasi liberalism in the 1970 Senate race against the conservative Democrat Lloyd Bentsen, and the 1971 flip-flop in defending and promoting the United Nations after having savaged it in 1964.

In 1980, in Bush's first presidential campaign, he won substantial support as a moderate Republican, and then without a word of protest or apology made the wholesale turnabouts—on abortion, "voodoo economics," right-wing politics, and much more—required to accept nomination as running mate to Ronald Reagan. Not only were these about-faces crucial to George Bush's later career, it's impossible to imagine him as president had he not been Reagan's vice president—though his eight years of abject loyalty to Reagan and frantic pursuit of conservative support lent a touch of comedy to the "wimp image" that nearly destroyed him.

The charge Bush repeatedly leveled against Clinton in 1992— that of "waffling"—might have been more appropriately pressed against Bush himself. What's to be said for a man who swung all the way from pro-choice in 1980 to hard-line antiabortion in 1988; who coined the phrase "voodoo economics," then supported its practice for eight years as the U.S. deficit ballooned; who could carry by his own moderate political efforts Republican primaries in states like Pennsylvania and Michigan in 1980, then seek the support of the far-right *Manchester Union-Leader* in the years to come?

To say of such episodes, "Oh, that's just politics," or "The chips were down, it had to be done," offers no real excuse; worse, it's condescending—an attitude into which George Bush's patrician background sometimes led him. Such drastic changes of position, such unrestrained attacks, are necessary only if winning an election is more important than personal probity; and "just politics" implies that different, lower standards of fairness and integrity may be applied if one is merely engaged in the grubby search for votes. George Bush on the tennis court never would have called "Out!" if an opponent's shot had clearly landed within the side- or baseline—that would have been cheating, beyond the bounds of decent behavior at Walker's Point or the Arundel Country Club. But "just politics" was something else, less demanding than honor on the playing field, with no bounds except winning.

So the same George H. W. Bush who would not cheat at games could repeatedly land low blows—negative ads, cheap shots, distorted facts—against mere political opponents like Dole or Dukakis, and contort his own positions into popular political shapes, and tell himself that this was fair behavior because it was "just politics."

"You can call it mud wrestling but I think it's fair to put it in focus," he said of his attack on Clinton's patriotism in the televised Richmond town meeting of 1992. In effect he was reminding the audience: "I'm of good family and good education with a long record of public service," the kind of person who would never cheat at golf or tennis—therefore he couldn't be fairly accused of

cheating in what he was saying in the debate (and anyway, that was different—just politics).

Bush also showed, however, on important questions, the virtues of his class—notably in 1974, when he advised President Nixon, to his face, to resign for the good of the Republican Party. For nearly two years, as the national party chairman, Bush had traveled the country tirelessly, insisting on the president's innocence, apparently believing in it wholeheartedly. Only the discovery and release of the "smoking gun" tape seems finally to have convinced Bush that Nixon had lied to him personally, to the Nixon family, to the nation, and to the Republicans who had upheld him loyally.

At that cabinet meeting on August 6, 1974, Bush seems to have acted out of true loyalty—not the ersatz variety so often practiced by self-protective politicians—when he rose uninvited to tell Nixon the truth "with the bark off": that it was necessary for the public, the presidency, and the country that Nixon should resign. That same day Barry Goldwater told Nixon he did not have enough remaining support in the Senate to survive an impeachment trial. The next day, August 7, Bush sent a personal letter to Nixon, again urging him to resign. On August 8, Nixon did.

Even at that tense moment in the cabinet room, however, it's possible that Bush, the experienced courtier, knew Nixon was going down and had a long eye on his own future. It's possible, but I believe rather that it was a moment of true patrician loyalty—it was *Nixon* who had let down the side, *Nixon* who was hurting the party and the presidency, *Nixon* who would have to go. Somebody had to tell him so, for the good of the team; and it was George Bush who recognized his duty to the team, at whatever personal cost or peril.

Perhaps it could be argued that, years later, in adopting so readily every particle of Ronald Reagan's right-wing policy, Bush again was "playing on the team"— at least as much as advancing his own future. And of course a vice president does owe his or her president a high degree of loyalty—which Bush certainly knew when he accepted a place on the ticket. But then he almost let himself disappear as a personality, within Reagan's shade; he swung, as noted, all the way to the right in his personal politics, he pursued the extremes of conservative support within the party, and he made no secret of his overriding ambition to succeed the Gipper in the White House. Nor is there a whit of evidence that he ever tried, as vice president, to move or influence the party toward something like the old "modern Republicanism" of Eisenhower and Prescott Bush. It might well have been political death to have done so, and his own political death was one thing George Bush avoided steadfastly.

The organization of Desert Storm represented another kind of team play—networking—that again would have been clearly identifiable at Walker's Point. In that autumn of 1990, George Bush called in all the international due bills he had been accumulating since 1970. Throughout his career, he had befriended men who in coming years would be the presidents and prime ministers and chiefs of staff and dictators who would answer the phone when President Bush called them from the White House.

He would be calling not those whom Lyndon Johnson considered subordinates, but men (and Margaret Thatcher) with whom George Bush had solid friendships, for whom in most cases he had personal respect. If you made lots of friends and were loyal to them, he'd been taught, they'd be loyal to you— most of the time anyway, and if sometimes they couldn't be,

George Bush was the kind of man who could understand the problem.

That fall and winter of 1990 and 1991 clearly marked the apex of his long career—and perhaps the one great thing (Desert Shield–Desert Storm) he did all by himself rather than as an executive relying on some one else's power and authority. There were Cheney and Powell and Schwartzkopf, of course, and the great military host they put together for him; and perhaps above all the sinuous James A. Baker III, backstopping Bush's skilled team playing with his own sure diplomatic and political touch.*

When Bush helicoptered down from Camp David on that momentous Sunday, August 5, 1990, however, and told reporters on the White House lawn that Saddam Hussein's invasion of Kuwait "will not stand," it was news to Colin Powell and probably to Baker too. That decision, Powell said in his memoir, had not been thrashed out in some high-level meeting where the blame or the credit could be spread around.[1] George Bush had made his decision—the most important of his nearly thirty years in politics—all alone.

It would be difficult to cite another such solitary conclusion in the public career of George Herbert Walker Bush. Powell tells us that the decisions to convert Desert Shield into Desert Storm,

*Since 1980, when Baker managed Bush's first presidential campaign, through most of the eighties, when he was Reagan's chief of staff, through his service as secretary of state in Bush's White House term, Baker was an invaluable associate. A decade later, when George W. Bush, "Junior," needed brilliant advocacy in the Florida vote imbroglio of 2000, he knew just where to turn—to a retired Jim Baker, still a brainier operator than anyone the other side could put up.

then to halt the latter short of the expulsion of Saddam Hussein from Iraq, were "staffed out," group decisions carefully calculated. Bush's green light for the assault on Bob Dole in 1988, and later for the raising of Michael Dukakis's negatives, all came under pressure from family and associates who assured him he would lose if he didn't follow their advice. The decision to focus in 1992 on whether Bill Clinton could be trusted, with the "womanizing draft dodger" charge visible in the background but never directly spoken, also came largely from aides, though it suited Bush's own inclinations (as an authentic World War II hero, he could hardly have viewed Clinton's draft avoidance during the war in Vietnam with anything but hostility).

Bush's long record in politics—two losing Senate races in Texas, one winning House campaign, and four unimposing years in the House (1967–71), as well as repeated presidential appointments—did not lead inevitably to the White House. On the other hand, owing to Bush's conspicuous loyalty and subservience to the powers he needed to please (save in the isolated instance of Nixon's resignation), his assiduous cultivation of friendships and family and political associations, and his nearly twenty years of uncomplaining willingness to wait for power, his political career did allow him plausibly to claim to be (though he never really was) Ronald Reagan's heir. And it was more as Reagan's vice president and supposed heir than by any claim of his own—as peacemaker? Cold Warrior? economic expertise?—that George Bush acceded to the Republican presidential nomination in 1988.

Even then, he had to resort to the most deplored and denounced campaign tactics of modern times to win his single term in the White House. During that term Bush did make the one decision—"this aggression will not stand"—on which rests any claim he has to having been a more notable president than most of those forgettable nineteenth-century suits who filled the White House slots between Washington, Jefferson, Jackson, Lincoln, and Theodore Roosevelt.

Ultimately, in the presidency, greatness is measured by decision making. "There stands the decision," John F. Kennedy wrote, perhaps with his wry gaze on himself, "and there stands the president." Ultimately, rarely, they may become one; the greatest decisions are arrived at not by careful, collective, staff review but by the instinct, backed by the knowledge and experience, of a commander—Lincoln recognizing a man "who fights" in appointing U.S. Grant to lead all federal armies at the climax of the Civil War; Franklin Roosevelt ("Dr. New Deal" becoming "Dr. Win-the-War") subtly preparing the nation for war in the thirties, when appeasement would have been more popular; Dwight Eisenhower refusing the determined advisers who wanted him to go to war to save the French in the Indochina of the fifties.

George Bush was rarely such a commander—perhaps not even as Desert Storm came to its disputed end in 1991, and certainly not in his fumbling leadership against an economic recession he scarcely recognized in 1990 and 1991. In his losing campaign against Bill Clinton in 1992, he seemed rattled and frustrated by his inability to raise the man's negatives, as he had Dukakis's in 1988—seeming to see no other course even in his desperation to hold on to the White House.

So perhaps we should return to where we began—with that old friend visiting a defeated but cheerful former president in the Houston replica of the Oval Office, finding "Poppy" Bush apparently with nothing more pressing to do than talk of old times. Perhaps the visitor had seen something real, so that his parting reflections raise essential questions about the life and presidency of George Herbert Walker Bush.

Even in the White House, did Bush have no more specific purposes than he had suggested in his years on the Andover board, no more pressing need than building and maintaining gracious relations with friends and colleagues around the world? Was George Bush only a nice man with good connections, who seldom had had to wrest from life the honors it frequently bestowed on him? Even if so, history has had worse things to say about many of those whose time it records. And if Desert Shield and Desert Storm are all but alone as monuments to the forty-first president, surely it can be said that they reflect moments of courage and vision worthy of his office.

Notes

CHAPTER ONE

1. Beschloss's essay on Bush, including this observation, is in Robert Wilson, ed., *Character Above All* (New York: Simon & Schuster, 1995), p. 224.
2. Richard Ben Cramer, *What It Takes* (New York: Random House, 1992; Vintage edition, 1993), p. 95.
3. George H. W. Bush with Victor Gold, *Looking Forward* (New York: Doubleday, 1987), p. 39.
4. Ibid., p. 44.
5. Ibid., p. 23.
6. Ibid., p. 46.
7. Cramer, *What It Takes*, p. 246.
8. The story of Zapata Petroleum's rise to fortune is based on the more detailed account in Cramer, *What It Takes*, pp. 146–47, a history largely confirmed in Bush, *Looking Forward*.
9. "I'd helped build a company from the ground up. . . . Politics is always in the air in Texas, and beginning in the late 1950s, I began to talk to close friends about my growing interest in public service." Bush, *Looking Forward*, p. 83.
10. Ibid., p. 88.
11. Beschloss, in Wilson, *Character Above All*, p. 229.
12. Bush, *Looking Forward*, p. 91.
13. Ibid., p. 5.
14. Ibid., p. 101.

15. Mark Hatfield, with the Senate Historical Office, *Vice Presidents of the United States, 1789–1993* (Washington, D.C.: U.S. Government Printing Office, 1997), p. 535.

CHAPTER TWO

1. George H. W. Bush, *All the Best* (New York: Scribner, 1999), p. 133. This is primarily a compilation of Bush's letters, interspersed with diary entries.
2. Ibid., pp. 132–33.
3. Bush, *Looking Forward*, pp. 110–11.
4. Ibid., pp. 111–12.
5. Bush, *All the Best*, p. 265.
6. Cramer, *What It Takes*, p. 611.
7. Bush, *Looking Forward*, p. 115.
8. Ibid., pp. 118–19.
9. Cramer, *What It Takes*, pp. 608–9.
10. Bush, *Looking Forward*, p. 123.
11. Ibid., pp. 122–25; Hatfield, *Vice Presidents of the United States*, p. 8.
12. Bush, *Looking Forward*, p. 122.
13. Ibid., pp. 131–49.
14. Bush, *All the Best*, pp. 209–10.
15. Ibid., p. 240.
16. Bush, *Looking Forward*, pp. 154, 159.
17. Ibid., p. 164.
18. Bush, *All the Best*, pp. 255, 257–59.
19. "Team B: The Trillion Dollar Experiment," the Internet version of an article in the *Bulletin of the Atomic Scientists*, April 1993.
20. Bush, *Looking Forward*, pp. 164–79; Bush, *All the Best*, p. 264.

CHAPTER THREE

1. Cramer, *What It Takes*, p. 791.
2. Bush, *All the Best*, pp. 270, 278.
3. The following account of the Reagan-Bush debate in New Hampshire in 1980, including all direct quotations, is compiled from

Bush, *Looking Forward,* pp. 199–202; Cramer, *What It Takes,* pp. 891–93; and Hatfield, *Vice Presidents of the United States,* pp. 10–11.

4. Bush, *Looking Forward,* p. 203.

5. Robert Scheer, *With Enough Shovels* (New York: Random House, 1982), pp. 29–30.

6. Cramer, *What It Takes,* pp. 579–80, 582.

7. Hatfield, *Vice Presidents of the United States,* p. 12.

8. Bush, *All the Best,* p. 303.

9. Bush, *Looking Forward,* p. 222.

10. Ibid., pp. 219–25.

11. www.colorado.edu/AmStudies/Lewis,2010/nuclear.htm, p. 8.

12. Cramer, *What It Takes,* p. 12.

13. Bush, *All the Best,* pp. 321–23.

14. Christopher Buckley, "Another March of Folly?" *New York Times,* Feb. 19, 2003, p. A 29.

15. Colin Powell, with Joseph E. Persico, *My American Journey* (New York: Random House, 1995), p. 375.

16. Bush, *All the Best,* pp. 339–40.

CHAPTER FOUR

1. Theodore Draper, *A Very Thin Line: The Iran-Contra Affairs* (New York: Hill and Wang, 1991), p. 133. The foregoing brief summaries of the origins of the "Iran-contra affair" are substantially based on Draper's heavily detailed accounts.

2. William S. Cohen and George Mitchell, *Men of Zeal* (New York: Viking, 1988), pp. 256–57. Cohen and Mitchell were the senior and junior U.S. senators from Maine, a Republican and a Democrat, and their book is based on the joint Senate-House hearings on the Iran-contra affair.

3. Draper, *A Very Thin Line,* pp. 248–49; Cohen and Mitchell, *Men of Zeal,* p. 265.

4. Jack W. Germond and Jules Witcover, *Mad as Hell: Revolt at the Ballot Box, 1992* (New York: Warner Books, 1993), p. 497.

5. Cohen and Mitchell, *Men of Zeal,* p. 265.

6. Ibid.

7. Ibid., pp. 271–72.

8. Ibid., pp. 266–67.

9. Bush, *Looking Forward,* p. 244.

10. Ibid., p. 240.

11. Cramer, *What It Takes,* pp. 115–17.

12. Cohen and Mitchell, *Men of Zeal,* pp. 264, 271.

13. Ibid., p. 272.

14. Cramer, *What It Takes,* p. 878.

15. Ibid., pp. 728–29.

16. Hatfield, *Vice Presidents of the United States,* p. 17.

17. Cramer, *What It Takes,* pp. 884–85.

CHAPTER FIVE

1. Cramer, *What It Takes,* p. 1011.

2. Ibid., p. 992.

3. Germond and Witcover, *Mad as Hell,* p. 25.

4. George Bush and Brent Scowcroft, *A World Transformed* (New York: Random House/Vintage, 1998), p. 20.

5. *Time* magazine, March 6, 1989, as reprinted in the *Time* archive on the Internet. This account of the Tower confirmation fight is based largely on the *Time* story and on my own recollection.

6. Ibid.

7. Germond and Witcover, *Mad as Hell,* p. 32.

CHAPTER SIX

1. Thomas Powers, *Intelligence Wars: American Secret History from Hitler to Al-Qaeda* (New York: New York Review of Books, 2002), p. 135.

2. Ibid., p. 284.

3. Bush and Scowcroft, *A World Transformed,* pp. 4–5.

4. Stephen White, *Communism and Its Collapse* (London and New York: Routledge, 2001), p. 35. White is a professor of politics at the University of Glasgow and the author of numerous books on Communism and the Soviet Union.

5. Bush and Scowcroft, *A World Transformed,* p. 132.

Notes

6. Ibid., p. 149.
7. Ibid., pp. 152–73.
8. Ibid., pp. 151, 155.
9. Bush, *All the Best*, pp. 542–43.

CHAPTER SEVEN

1. Powers, *Intelligence Wars*, pp. 327–28, quoting Robert Gates, *From the Shadows: The Ultimate Insider's Story of Five Presidents and How They Won the Cold War* (New York: Simon & Schuster, 1996).
2. Bush and Scowcroft, *A World Transformed*. Both quotations are on p. 300.
3. This account of events leading up to Operation Just Cause and its execution is derived from a detailed article by Eytan Gilboa in *Political Science Quarterly* 110 (no. 4), 1995, p. 539; and from the *West Point Atlas of Major Conflicts*, both to be found at www.military.com/resources.
4. Bush and Scowcroft, *A World Transformed*, p. 305.
5. For a detailed account of U.S. support for Iraq in the 1980s, see Michael Dobbs, "U.S. Had Key Role in Iraq Buildup," *Washington Post*, December 30, 2002, p. A1.
6. Bush and Scowcroft, *A World Transformed*, p. 330.
7. Ibid., p. 326.
8. Powell, *My American Journey*, p. 453.
9. Nathan J. Brown, "PG War," Microsoft Encarta online encyclopedia, 2003. Brown is associate dean, Elliott School of International Affairs, George Washington University.
10. Powell, *My American Journey*, pp. 456–75.
11. Ibid., pp. 463–65.
12. Ibid., p. 477.
13. Bush and Scowcroft, *A World Transformed*, p. 456.

1. Powell, *My American Journey*, p. 485.
2. www.cryan.com/war/.

3. Ibid. U.S. estimates are that one hundred thousand Iraqi soldiers died, three hundred thousand were wounded, one hundred fifty thousand deserted, and sixty thousand were captured. Actual figures may have been much higher.

4. "[O]ur Arab allies . . . now trusted us more than they ever had. We had come to their assistance . . . asked nothing for ourselves, and [would leave] when the job was done." Bush and Scowcroft, *A World Transformed,* p. 490.

5. This summary of the end of the Gulf War is derived from Powell, *My American Journey,* and from Nathan J. Brown, *Persian Gulf War,* www/encarta.msn.com. The reasons the Bush administration left Saddam Hussein in power in an uninvaded Iraq are discussed at length by General Powell.

6. Bush and Scowcroft, *A World Transformed,* p. 489.

7. Bush, *All the Best,* p. 548.

8. Germond and Witcover, *Mad as Hell,* p. 368.

CHAPTER NINE

1. The full text of Buchanan's speech can be found at www.buchanan.org/pa-92-0817-rnc.html.

2. According to Germond and Witcover in *Mad as Hell.*

3. Ibid. pp. 413, 416.

4. This remark was confirmed by Jordan in a personal letter to me.

CHAPTER TEN

1. Powell, *My American Journey,* p. 453.

Sources

MOSTLY the notes tell the story. But, to summarize briefly, I depended heavily on three books by George Bush himself and collaborators: *Looking Forward,* a campaign biography written with Victor Gold (New York: Doubleday, 1987); *All the Best,* a book compiled from Bush's letters and diary (New York: Scribner, 1999); and *A World Transformed,* written jointly (in alternate passages) by Bush and his former national security adviser, Brent Scowcroft (New York: Random House/Vintage, 1998).

Other major book sources include *What It Takes,* about the 1988 campaign, by Richard Ben Cramer (New York: Random House/Vintage, 1993); *Vice Presidents of the United States, 1789–1993,* by former senator Mark Hatfield of Oregon, with the Senate Historical Office (Washington, D.C.: U.S. Government Printing Office, 1997); *With Enough Shovels,* by Robert Scheer (New York: Random House, 1982); *My American Journey,* by Colin Powell, with Joseph E. Persico (New York: Random House, 1995); *A Very Thin Line: The Iran-Contra Affairs,* by Theodore Draper (New York: Hill and Wang, 1991); *Men of Zeal,* by former senators William S. Cohen, Republican of Maine, and George Mitchell, Democrat of Maine, about the joint congressional hearings on the Iran-contra affair (New York: Viking, 1988); *Whose Broad Stripes and Bright Stars,* about the 1988 campaign, and *Mad as Hell,* about the 1992 campaign, both by Jack W. Germond and Jules Witcover (New York: Warner Books, 1989 and 1993); *Intelligence Wars*, by Thomas Powers (New York: New York Review of Books, 2002); and *Communism and Its Collapse*, by Stephen White (London and New York: Routledge, 2001).

I also received much help from Internet sources, sometimes in ways I found difficult to footnote, but particularly from the *Time* magazine archive and articles from *Political Science Quarterly*, the *Bulletin of the Atomic Scientists*, and the *West Point Atlas of Major Conflicts*. An article by Michael Beschloss, in *Character Above All*, edited by Robert Wilson (New York: Simon & Schuster, 1995), was particularly helpful (in the same book I provided an analysis of Richard Nixon, and that book was the basis for a public television hour on the presidency in about 1996).

Of course, there are numerous references to G. H. W. Bush in books too numerous to list. One of my best sources was my own memory, since as a reporter I covered much of the activity discussed in these pages. I could not rely on memory for specifics—such as dates—but I could and did recall the general atmosphere of a time and an event, such as a presidential campaign or a televised debate.

The opening anecdote, or prologue, is based on a private conversation with a close friend; I showed the version in the manuscript to that person and he approved of it after first insisting on a rewrite to make clear that Bush was a popular and willing—but not very creative—member of the Andover board.